CW01477020

# Discovered Lives:
## Ladies of St Giles', Edinburgh
### 1587-1672

Rosalind K. Marshall

Rosalind K. Marshall Publishing, Edinburgh

© Rosalind K. Marshall 2019

British Library Cataloguing-in Publication Data:
A catalogue record for this book is available from the British Library

ISBN 978-1-5272-4717-8

Typeset by Victoria Arrowsmith-Brown
Printed by 4Word Ltd, Page & Print Production
Distributed by Arrowsmith

# Contents

# List of Illustrations

# Note

I have modernised archaic spellings for ease of reading. As for currency, in the mid-sixteenth century £1 Scots was worth one quarter of the English £1 sterling, but by 1603 its value had fallen to one-twelfth of £1 sterling and it remained at that level until 1707, when the separate coinage disappeared with the Act of Union. A merk was worth thirteen shillings and four pence Scots. A shilling was worth one-twentieth of a pound and a penny was worth one-twelfth of a shilling.

# Reference Abbreviations

**Brunton,** *Lords of Session* – George Brunton and David Haig, *An Historical Account of the Senators of the College of Justice of Scotland* (Edinburgh 1832; The Making of Modern Law edition, 2010)

*CSPScot 1589-1593* – *Calendar of the State Papers relating to Scotland and Mary, Queen of Scots*, 1589-1593, edd. William K. Boyd and Henry W. Meikle (Edinburgh 1936); ibid. 1593-1595, ed. Annie Cameron (Edinburgh 1936); ibid. 1547-1603, ed. J.D. Mackie (Edinburgh 1969)

**ECA, Dean of Guild Accounts 1568-1626, 1626-1720** – Edinburgh City Archives, manuscript volumes 1568-626, 1626-1720 (The pagination of these two large volumes does not run from beginning to end. Small groups of pages for, say, one year, are paginated, others are not, so the user should look first for the year concerned, e.g. '1626-27' and then read through it for specific entries)

**Edinburgh Burgh Extracts** – *Extracts from the Records of the Burgh of Edinburgh, 1403-1655*, ed. Marguerite Wood et al. (Edinburgh 1869-1938)

***Edinburgh Housemails Taxation Book*** – *Edinburgh Housemails Taxation Book 1634-1636*, edd. Aaron Allen and Cathryn Spence (Scottish History Society 2014)

***Handbook of British Chronology*** – ed. F.M. Powicke and E.B. Fryde (London 1961)

***Lamont's Diary*** – *The Diary of Mr John Lamont of Newton 1649-1671*, ed. *George R. Kinloch* (Maitland Club 1830)

***Lord Provosts of Edinburgh*** – *The Lord Provosts of Edinburgh 1296-1932*, ed. Marguerite Wood (Edinburgh 1932)

***ODNB*** – *Oxford Dictionary of National Biography* (Oxford University Press 2004)

***Scot of Scotstarvet*** – Sir John Scot, *The Staggering State of Scottish Statesmen from 1550 to 1650*, ed. Charles Rogers (Edinburgh 1872, Naba Public Domain Reprints)

***Scots Peerage*** – *The Scots Peerage*, ed. Sir James Balfour Paul (Edinburgh 1904-14)

# Acknowledgements

I thank all those who have encouraged my pursuit of the elusive women of late sixteenth and early seventeenth century Scotland, arising from my desire to discover and understand their attitudes and experiences in times very different from our own. In writing this book I have been particularly grateful to generations of families, librarians and archivists who have carefully preserved the letters and accounts of those long departed female forbears, allowing us to catch a glimpse of their often challenging daily lives. In particular, I should like to thank the staff of Edinburgh City Archives, Dr Frances Shaw, the National Records of Scotland, the National Galleries of Scotland, the Tate Gallery, London, Dunedin Art Gallery, New Zealand, the Trustees of the Lauderdale Aisle in St Mary's Church, Haddington, Mrs Alison Meikle, Session Clerk of St Mary's, and Steve Lister, Operations Manager at Greyfriars Kirk, Edinburgh, David Forsyth and Margaret Wilson of the National Museum of Scotland, while Peter Backhouse went out of his way to take his characteristically excellent photographs for the present day illustrations. Victoria Arrowsmith-Brown and 4Word saw the book through press. I am grateful to them all.

R.K.M.

25 September 2019

# Foreword

## by the Very Reverend Dr Gilleasbuig Macmillan KCVO

This book is a fascinating collection of the ladies who were connected to St Giles' around five hundred years ago. Sources of information about the beliefs and reactions of such women of the past are too brief to provide us with complete biographies, but using the available documentation, the author carries our minds and imaginations on a journey to Scotland and life in those days, especially in Edinburgh. Glimpses are not to be despised. An individual may make a strong impact from one brief meeting, with no requirement for the full picture to be given to us, just as the sight of a mountain on a day when the light and the snow are 'right' can make an impact which is perfectly sufficient and needs no filling in.

Here the personalities of these ladies are lit up with just enough information; set in their times with its great houses and continuing titles, the overlapping of the Reformed Church with older ways, and all linked to their seating in St Giles'. In a way reminiscent of such an experience I find Dr Marshall's Ladies delightfully indicative of the town and the great church of Edinburgh.

Gilleasbuig Macmillan

# Introduction

The century after the Reformation of 1560 was a time of turmoil in Scotland. Not only did people have to adjust to the new ways of worship, but in 1603 the royal Court moved to London when King James VI inherited the throne of England. After that came opposition to royal financial and ecclesiastical policies, civil war and Oliver Cromwell's military occupation of Scotland, followed by the Restoration of Charles II in 1660. Of course important men feature in histories of the period, but all too often wives are ignored, at best meriting no more than a sentence or two in their husbands' biographies. So how can we find out about the experiences and reactions of women during those significant decades?

This is a challenging task, because of the scarcity of documentary evidence. A favourite anecdote, popularised by Sir Walter Scott, tells how the semi-apocryphal Jenny Geddes started a riot in 1637 by throwing her stool at Dean Hannay in St Giles' Cathedral when he began to read from Charles I's new English-style prayer book, considered by many to presage a return to Roman Catholicism.[1] No reliable details of her life have ever been discovered, and this is not surprising because few even of the elite women were taught to write until the early seventeenth century. They learned to read, so that they could study their Bibles, but the papers of those who were fully literate were all too often discarded after their deaths because their descendants were focused on preserving title deeds and other legal documents.

In trying to discover more about those women who were close to the centre of events during these troubled years, it is worth looking to Edinburgh for an answer. Although the royal Court had departed, after 1603 the Scottish Parliament and the Scottish Privy Council remained in the capital, along with the principal law courts. As a result, influential office holders, leading lawyers and the wealthy merchants who engaged in foreign trade were based there with their families, even if they also owned properties in the country. No reliable population statistics for the period exist, but it is generally accepted that in the 1590s about 15,000 people were living in Edinburgh, the number rising to around 20,000-25,000 by 1635 and then slowing down again towards the end of the century because of outbreaks of the plague.[2] Rich and poor alike lived in close proximity to each other in what is now the centre of the Old Town, the wealthy owning or renting houses there.

Unfortunately, there was no such thing as a census in those days, so how can we discover the names of the women who were at the centre of Edinburgh society? At the heart of the High Street stood and stands the medieval church of St Giles', which became a cathedral in 1633 on the orders of Charles I. Now it might be supposed that its archives would provide us with lists of those who worshipped there, but unfortunately no congregational registers have survived for the period under consideration. This is a pity, but such lists usually noted households only under the name of the chief member, normally the husband or father, without mentioning the women of the family, and therefore from our point of view this is not a major loss.

Fortunately a valuable source of the information that we need exists in Edinburgh City Archives.

The St Giles' building was actually owned by the town and the Town Council's Dean of Guild was responsible for its upkeep. Apart from seeing to the endless repairs to its constantly leaking roof, he had to organise all manner of changes to the interior. For example, before the Reformation, no seating had been required, because at Mass the homily given by the officiating priest was brief, but after 1560 the Reformed services included a sermon from the minister which lasted for an hour at the very least. As a result, the Town Council ordered the Dean of Guild to have seats, forms and stools made, 'for the people to sit upon, the time of the sermon and prayers', and initially during the early years men and women were segregated so that they would not distract one another during the services.'[3]

From the very start, despite the fact that everyone was regarded as being equal before God, prominent men were given their own seats in balconies known as lofts, specially constructed for them. King James VI, for instance, was not born until six years after the Reformation, but when he was old enough to attend services he sat in his elaborately carved, gilded and painted Royal Loft and there were also special lofts for noblemen, the Court of Session judges and the Town Council of Edinburgh. Of course, ambitious members of the congregation who were not granted places in a loft soon started to demand special seats of their own. Seat rents were introduced by 1640, whereby members who paid a sum of money in advance were able to reserve a seat for a year, the proceeds going towards the ministers' stipends, but that did not interest those who wanted something more imposing.[4] The desire to see and be seen was as prevalent then as it has been in later centuries.

Crucially from our point of view, some of the women whose husbands occupied lofts also wanted their own special seats. They, or their husbands on their behalf, had to apply to the Town Council and, if their request was granted, the Dean of Guild ordered the seat's construction. We do not know what these seats looked like, but presumably they were grander and more noticeable than those supplied for ordinary members of the congregation. It is recorded that the pulpit and the fronts of the lofts had draperies of green cloth, with silk fringes, and the Provost sat upon a special cushion on his special chair, which was upholstered in green, so perhaps the ladies' special seats had some similar signs of importance.

The most sought after positions were near the King's Loft and the Town Council loft, because that was where the Lord Provost sat and there was a good view of the pulpit. The number of applications from leading women noticeably increased when James VI's return visit to Scotland in 1617 was imminent and likewise in the lengthy prelude to Charles I's Scottish coronation in 1633 which, it was thought, might take place in St Giles' but was eventually held at Holyrood Abbey instead.[5]

Another result of the Reformation had been that with the removal of the Roman Catholic altars and other furnishings, the interior of St Giles' had become a vast preaching hall, far too big for any minister, even John Knox, to be able to make himself heard, and so stone partition walls were built to divide up the space. In 1586 the former chancel became the completely self-contained East Kirk, while the crossing and part of the nave were now called the Auld Kirk and in 1598 an area at the north-west end became

4

the Tolbooth Kirk. The East Kirk was apparently the most fashionable. A year after it opened, the Town Council were noting that the throng of people coming to its services was so large that the minister had great difficulty in getting to the pulpit.[6]

Of course most people could not choose which church to attend, for they were assigned to it according to the parish in which they lived. That said, the Town Council, the Lords of Session and some prominent individuals were allowed to have seats in two of the churches, and those who were favoured in this way included some of the influential women. Whatever the location of the special seats, the cost was borne by the town and was noted in the Dean of Guild's account books. The two account books for our period, preserved in Edinburgh City Archives, are therefore valuable historical sources.

Given the names of those women who achieved their own seats, we can then look for further information about them.[7] Did they lead pampered and privileged lives, free from any troubles, economic or emotional? They came from different parts of Scotland, their marriages had been arranged for them, often with no consideration for their feelings, and some of them rarely saw their own relatives again. Many of them spent the next twenty years or so having children, a third of whom would not survive, and legally they were expected to be obedient to their husbands in all things. Only once they were widowed could they then marry a man of their own choice. Did that mean that they were meek, downtrodden individuals, without any opportunity to express their opinions or influence their family and friends? Not so. No one can know what they thought as they sat listening to the sermons in St Giles' but, having now identified them, we can in other sources catch a glimpse of their personalities, their marital relationships and their reactions to the challenging events of their time.

---

[1] David Stevenson, 'Jenny Geddes, supposed religious activist', *ODNB*, (Oxford University Press, 2004)

[2] Michael Lynch, *Edinburgh and the Reformation* (Edinburgh 1981), 11-14

[3] *Edinburgh Burgh Extracts 1557-1571*, ii, 67

[4] Ibid., 1626-41, 243

[5] Edinburgh City Archives, MS Dean of Guild Accounts 1568-1626; 1626-1720 (SL144/4/3,4)

[6] *Edinburgh Burgh Extracts 1573-1589*, 496

[7] Three of the women remain elusive, for it has not proved possible to discover the precise identities of Mrs Alexander Maybie (1628), Lady Birnie (1631-32) or Lady Martine (1631-32)

# 1

## *Jean Fleming, Lady Thirlestane*

Jean Fleming is the first woman to be mentioned in the records as having her own seat in Edinburgh's parish church of St Giles'. That was in 1587 when, six days after her husband had been made Lord Chancellor of Scotland, the Dean of Guild was ordered by the Town Council to make a seat for her in the East Kirk, in a place which 'she shall find most commodious'.[1] Hers had been a relatively late marriage, for although Jean was the only child of James, 4th Lord Fleming, he had died in 1558 when she was only four years old and she was left without the tocher (dowry) necessary before someone of her status could marry. Her father had made provision for that, but in 1579 Jean was successfully complaining to the Scottish Privy Council that she had never been provided with her promised 4000 merks Scots. Only after she was also awarded in 1583 some property from her grandfather's estate was she able to marry Sir John Maitland of Lethington, the most powerful politician in Scotland. She was 29 and he was a bachelor of 39.[2]

Together, they were at the centre of the Court of James VI, for this was before the King inherited the English throne in 1603 and moved to London. Maitland came from a family of poets, was a poet himself, and Jean seems to have been better educated than many Scotswomen of the time, for when her seat was erected in St Giles' in 1587, the wright was told to supply an extra piece of wood 'to lay her books on'. Even other aristocratic women of the period owned fewer than a dozen volumes. That same year, the ambitious Scottish poet William Fowler dedicated to her his translation of Petrarch's famous poem 'Trionfi' (Triumphs), comparing her to its heroine, Laura.[3] Fowler genuinely admired Jean's abilities and considered her to be highly influential, telling Lord Burghley the English statesman in 1589 that she was a wise woman, 'and half Chancellor when he [her husband] was at home'.[4]

The following year, at the coronation of James VI's new wife, Anne of Denmark, Jean walked in procession behind her, becoming for a time her close friend, while Maitland was raised to the peerage as Lord Thirlestane.[5] Their position seemed unassailable, but in 1592 the manoeuvrings of his enemies led to Maitland's dismissal from Court, and the couple divided their time between their houses of Lethington (the present day Lennoxlove) and Thirlestane. Failing in health, Jean's husband made his Will on 31 August 1595, nominating his 'dearest spouse' as his executor. She was also to be guardian of their two children, Anne and John, who were still minors, and he begged the King to be 'a careful protector and defender of them'. He died at Thirlestane on 3 October that year.[6] Despite his fall from favour, he had remained as Chancellor but after his death the position was not filled for another four years, with the result that the Dean of Guild accounts continued to refer to Jean as 'the Lady Chancellor'. She went on attending services at St Giles' and by 1596 she had an additional seat under James VI's loft, which was in the Auld Kirk. This was a favoured position because of its proximity to the monarch and its excellent view of the minister.[7]

As a wealthy widow, Jean could have chosen to remain single, but in November 1597, at the age of 43 and to the ribald amusement of the entire Court, she suddenly married John, 5th Earl of Cassillis. He was 29. Whatever her motivation, his was clear. He wanted her fortune, and as she sat in St Giles' she may have enjoyed her enhanced status as a Countess. As time went by, however, she probably regretted her choice. Her second husband was always petulant, constantly falling out with relatives and neighbours and in 1604 he horrified everyone by assaulting Jean and dragging her out of the Privy Council Chamber at Holyroodhouse in a public quarrel with her about a lease. Shocked at reports of the incident, James VI ordered Cassillis to be imprisoned for a time in Blackness Castle and then give £5000 security for his wife's protection.[8]

We know that Jean was still going to St Giles' on a Sunday and taking books with her, for in 1607-8 David Brown the wright supplied a desk for her beside her stall in the East Kirk at a cost of £3:14/-. A desk was becoming the normal accompaniment for important seats. He made it in his own premises at a cost of £3:2/- and then charged the Town Council 2 shillings and three pence for carrying it 'up the gaitt [street] to the Kirk'. John Stewart painted it for £3:6/- and Thomas Duncan, smith, provided a lock, key and bands to it, charging £2:10/-.[9] Not long afterwards, on 22 June 1609, Jean died after a long illness, leaving the impressive sum of over £3000 Scots.[10] She was buried beside her first husband in the Maitland family vault in St Mary's Church, Haddington, where the elaborate monument with their alabaster effigies is a prominent feature. (Plate 4) The accompanying Latin epitaph praises her serenity, adding that her 'manly spirit' had remained constant in times of both success and uncertainty and she 'displayed to the highest degree piety towards God.'[11]

How true was that? In 1602, at a time when James VI had offended his Protestant subjects by giving his small daughter, Princess Elizabeth, into the keeping of the Catholic Lady Livingston, an English observer had remarked that the Countess of Cassillis would be more acceptable, being a lady without all religion. This sounds like a piece of gossip, for the records of Jean's seating in St Giles' over the years suggest otherwise, indicating instead a continuing spiritual commitment.[12] Cassillis survived her, dying in 1615.[13]

---

[1] *Edinburgh Burgh Extracts 1604-1626*, 497; *Handbook of British Chronology*, 176; ECA, MS Dean of Guild Accounts 1568-1626, 292

[2] *Scots Peerage*, viii, 542-3; Marcus Merriman, 'Fleming, James, 4th Lord Fleming', *ODNB* (Oxford University Press 2004); *Edinburgh Burgh Extracts 1604-26*, 333

[3] S. M. Dunnigan, 'Fowler, William' *ODNB* (Oxford University Press 2004); T. Van Heijnsbergen, 'Coteries, commendatory verse and Jacobean poetics; William Fowler's Triumphs of Petrarke and its Castalian Circles' in *James VI and I, Literature and Scotland: Tides of Change, 1567-1625*, (Leuven 2013), 45-63; Sebastiaan Verweij, *The Literary Culture of Early Modern Scotland: Manuscript Production and Transmission, 1560-1625* (Oxford University Press, 2016)

[4] *Calendar of the Cecil Papers in Hatfield House*, iii, 1583-1589 (H.M.S.O. 1889), no. 948, 447

[5] *CSPScot* xi, ed. Annie I. Cameron (Edinburgh 1936), 539, 594, 598; Maureen M. Meikle, 'Anna of Denmark's Coronation and Entry into Edinburgh, 1590' in *Sixteenth Century Scotland, Essays in Honour of Michael Lynch*, ed. Julian Goodare and Alasdair A. MacDonald (Leiden 2008), 285; Maurice Lee jun., 'Maitland, John, 1st Lord Maitland of Thirlestane', *ODNB* (Oxford University Press 2004)

[6] *CSPScot* x, ed. William K. Boyd and Henry W. Meikle (Edinburgh 1936), 793; NRS, Wills and Testaments, Edinburgh Commissary Court, CC8/8/33/223-229; 'Maitland, John, Lord Thirlestane', *ODNB* (Oxford University Press 2004)

[7] ECA, MS Dean of Guild Accounts 1568-1626, 644

[8] *Scots Peerage*, ii, 475-7; *CSPScot 1547-1603*, 125; Sharon Adams, 'Fleming, Jean, Countess of Cassillis', *ODNB* (Oxford University Press 2004)

[9] *Edinburgh Burgh Extracts 1604-1626*, 333

[10] NRS, Wills and Testaments, Edinburgh Commissary Court, CC8/8/46/208-209 (Jean Fleming)

[11] Lauderdale Monument, St Mary's Church, Haddington, with effigies of Jean and her husband on the left. See Plate 5. Translation of the Latin epitaph by Roy Pinkerton

[12] *CSPScot 1547-1603*, xiii, 125, 997; ECA, MS Dean of Guild Accounts 1568-1626, 176, 615, 644; 1607-1608, n/p; *Edinburgh Burgh Extracts 1604-26*, 333

[13] *Scots Peerage*, ii, 477

# 2

## *Eleanor Musgrave, Mrs Bowes*

In June 1592, Elizabeth I of England's ambassador to Scotland, the long-suffering Robert Bowes, was provided by Edinburgh's Dean of Guild with a splendid new feather cushion of tawny English velvet trimmed with silk tassels and lace. This would lie on the front ledge of his loft in St Giles', so that he could rest his arms on it, as was the custom. On weekdays, the little cushion would be stored in a special buckram case. Intriguingly, a matching cushion was provided for Eleanor Musgrave, his wife. Unusually, the couple must have been sitting together in the same loft.[1]

Eleanor was the daughter of Sir Richard Musgrave of Eden Hall, Cumberland, and her husband came from Aske, in the Richmond district of North Yorkshire. They had married in 1566, when she was twenty and he was a widower with at least one young son. Apart from property in Yorkshire, they had a house in Berwick, where Bowes became Treasurer in 1576.[2] Because of his geographical proximity to Scotland, he was regularly sent to Edinburgh by Elizabeth I as her ambassador. Interestingly, his now deceased sister Marjorie had been the wife of the famous Reformer John Knox, first minister of St Giles' after the Reformation.[3]

Eleanor, who had no children of her own, accompanied Bowes on his thankless missions, undeterred by an unfortunate incident in 1578 when William Robesoun, a slater's servant, attacked and injured her. No details of the assault are known, but Robesoun was sentenced to be bound to a gibbet and have his tongue pierced before being banished from Edinburgh.[4] On a happier note, at the coronation of Anne of Denmark at Holyroodhouse in 1590, Eleanor was one of the four ladies carrying her long train.[5] The young James VI was now ruling for himself, so her husband's diplomatic role gradually diminished, and he died Berwick, on 16 December 1597.

Hoping to succeed him as ambassador, Henry Lok, an English poet and minor intelligencer, dedicated a poetic version of the biblical Book of Ecclesiastes to Elizabeth I, attaching to it sixty sonnets addressed to influential people. Most of the twenty women included were countesses and ladies-in-waiting to the English Queen, but the last was 'Mistress E. Bowes'. The reason for Eleanor's inclusion was obvious in view of Lok's ambition to succeed Bowes, but it also suggests that she was well known to Elizabeth I. Unfortunately for Lok, his initiative was unsuccessful.[6]

After her husband's death Eleanor retired to their manor house of Great Broughton in Yorkshire, but although she had not been a parishioner of Robert Bruce, who became minister of St Giles' after her time in Edinburgh, she did try to help him in 1601. An outspoken critic of James VI's ecclesiastical policies, Bruce was in constant trouble with the King and was not only banished from St Giles' but forced into exile. However, he visited Eleanor in the north of England on his way back, and she intervened on his behalf. Whether this had any effect is uncertain, but Bruce was allowed to return to Scotland a few months later.[7]

During her retirement, Eleanor attended St Agatha's Church in Easby, where she was well-known for her philanthropy. In 1607 she founded the Bowes Hospital in Richmond as an almshouse for three poor widows,[8] subsequently bequeathing money for their bedding, furniture, and gowns. Her carved initials and coat of arms still survive on the building, and her bequests included £40 for poor tradesmen in the town, provided they supplied coal for her Hospital. She added a stern second condition which throws light on her views. None of the money was to be given to 'a Popish recusant', a non-communicant or anyone involved in a gross, scandalous or disorderly life unless there was evidence that they had truly reformed.[9]

As she rested her arms on her velvet cushion in St Giles' in her more youthful days, the sermons Eleanor heard there must have accorded with her own outlook on life. She finally died on 25 July 1623 at the age of 77 and was buried in St Agatha's Church, where she is commemorated by the oldest surviving brass plaque in the chancel.[10]

---

[1] *Edinburgh Burgh Extracts 1604-26*, 66, 344

[2] C. A. McGladdery, 'Bowes, Robert', *ODNB* (Oxford University Press 2004)

[3] *The Works of John Knox*, ed. D. Laing (Wodrow Society, Edinburgh 1854), lxiii-lxxv; Rosalind K. Marshall, *John Knox* (Edinburgh 2000), 188, 214

[4] *Edinburgh Burgh Extracts 1573-1589*, 73

[5] Maureen M. Meikle, 'Anna of Denmark's Coronation and Entry into Edinburgh, 1590' in *Sixteenth Century Scotland, Essays in Honour of Michael Lynch*, ed. Julian Goodare and Alasdair A. MacDonald (Leiden 2008)

[6] James Doleman, 'Seeking "The Fruit of Favour": The Dedicatory Sonnets of Henry Lok's *Ecclesiastes*' in *English Literary History*, (John Hopkins University Press 1993), vol. 60, 1-15

[7] *The Acts and Proceedings of the General Assemblies of the Church of Scotland 1587-1618* ed. Duncan Shaw (Scottish Record Society 2004), ii, 1286-1290

[8] *A History of the County of York North Riding* ed. William Page (Victoria County History, London 1914), 17-35

[9] Christopher Clarkson, *The History of Richmond, in the County of York* (Richmond 1821), 228-229

[10] *The Correspondence of Robert Bowes of Aske, Esquire, The Ambassador of Queen Elizabeth in the Court of* Scotland (Surtees Society, London 1842) p. ix; Historic England, *[tps://historicengland.org.uk/listing/the-list-list-entry/1289900*

# 3

## *Lilias Drummond, Lady Fyvie*

Lilias Drummond was the second daughter of Patrick, 3rd Lord Drummond and his wife Lady Elizabeth Lindsay. Born in the late 1570s, she had two brothers and four sisters. Little is known about her father's career, other than the fact that he seems to have been in major financial difficulties for much of his life. When his wife died in 1585, he married again, with the result that Lilias and her siblings acquired a mature and influential stepmother.[1] Agnes Drummond was an illegitimate daughter of King James IV and she had already been married twice. She had four children, all adults by the time she became the wife of Lilias's father, who may have been a distant relative.[2] When Agnes herself died in 1590, she left many bequests of furnishings to her husband, but the executor of her Testament was to be her son-in-law, Robert Seton, 6th Lord Seton.[3] Two years later, Lilias was married to his younger brother, Alexander Seton. He was thirty-six, and Lilias would have been about fifteen at the time.

Her husband had an interesting past. He had been a godson of Mary, Queen of Scots and his father, George, 5th Lord Seton, a staunch Roman Catholic and one of the exiled Queen's most loyal supporters, had sent him to Rome in 1571 to study at the Jesuit German College, with the intention that he should enter the priesthood. There he studied Greek, Latin and Mathematics and his outstanding abilities were soon recognised. However, he was well aware of the difficulty of finding a career in newly

Reformed Scotland and so he changed course, moving to Paris to study Law. Home again, he became a successful advocate and gained the favour of James VI, who was beginning his personal reign.

When Seton was appointed as a Lord of Session in 1588, his rivals were quick to accuse him of being a Catholic, alleging that he had indeed become a priest during his time in Rome. The Reformed community in general seized upon the fact that he never attended Communion as he ought to do. In order to deflect criticism and save his career, he decided that he would conform publicly, while remaining privately faithful to the Catholic Church.[4] It was against this background that in 1591 he married the Protestant Lilias, presumably in the hope of reassuring his opponents that he too genuinely belonged to the Reformed Church. A year later, she gave birth to their first daughter, Anne, followed by Isobel, in 1593. Margaret, born in 1596, died in infancy but a second Margaret came along in 1599.[5] She was baptised in St Giles' on 8 August, with the Lord Treasurer, John, 5th Earl of Cassillis and four of the town bailies attending as official witnesses.[6] Finally there was Sophia.

Meanwhile, supported by the King, Seton's career was advancing rapidly. In 1593 he was appointed President of the Court of Session and chairman of a committee managing the properties belonging to James VI's young wife, Anne of Denmark. The Queen was also Seton's patron, and Lilias's sister Jean Drummond was Anne's favourite lady-in-waiting, so the family were very much at the centre of the royal Court. In 1598 Lilias became Lady Fyvie when the King bestowed on her husband the position of a Lord of Parliament and then, despite considerable opposition, had him elected as Provost of Edinburgh, a position that he would hold for ten years.[7]

It was in 1600, as the Lord Provost's wife, that Lilias was granted her own seat in St Giles'[8] and at the end of that year she and Seton received a very great honour. On 19 November James VI's younger son, the future Charles I, was born at his mother's palace of Dunfermline, and in keeping with the usual security measures of the time, to avoid having the monarch and his heirs living in the same place, the King decreed that the little Prince should be brought up in the care of Lord and Lady Fyvie.[9] Anne of Denmark was bitterly opposed to being separated from her children and it is possible that James hoped that she would be reconciled to losing Charles since he was going to a couple she knew well and would be living in their household close to Dunfermline Palace.

The baby was duly given into their care, only for Lilias to die soon afterwards, on 8 May 1601 in their home at Dalgety. She was buried in the family vault which her husband had built at St Bridget's Church there. He eventually registered her Testament as her executor on 16 January 1609. Fyvie Castle and its lands had been settled on her and as well as the crops and livestock there, she left jewellery, clothing, silver and goldsmith work to the value of 6000 merks.[10] Lord Fyvie went on to become 1st Earl of Dunfermline and Lord Chancellor of Scotland, marrying twice more **(4) (15)**. Lilias, for her part, has gained a strange and entirely fictitious fame as 'The Green Lady', a ghost who energetically carved her name on the stone windowsill of one of the bedchambers in Fyvie Castle, where she is mistakenly said to have died, starved to death by her husband. There is no truth in that at all, except for the fact that her carved name can still be seen there.

---

[1] *Scots Peerage*, vii, 47

[2] Ibid., iii, 440-442

[3] NRAS, Wills and Testaments, Edinburgh Commissary Court, CC8/8/26/199-204 (Agnes Drummond)

[4] Michael Lynch, 'Seton, George, 5th Lord Seton', *ODNB* (Oxford University Press 2004); Maurice Lee Jr, 'Seton, Alexander, first earl of Dunfermline' in ibid.; Brunton, *Lords of Session,* 198-199

[5] *Scots Peerage,* iii, 372

[6] George Seton, *Memoir of Alexander Seton, Earl of Dunfermline* (Edinburgh 1882), 150-151, 153, n.1

[7] Lee, "Seton, Alexander, first earl of Dunfermline", *ODNB* (Oxford University Press 2004); *Lord Provosts of Edinburgh,* 33-34

[8] ECA, MS Dean of Guild Accounts, 1568-1626, p.767

[9] Mark A. Kishlansky and John Morrill, 'Charles I', *ODNB* (Oxford University Press 2004)

[10] NRS, Wills and Testaments, Edinburgh Commissary Court, CC8/8/44/635-637 (Lilias Drummond)

# 4

## *Grizel Leslie, Countess of Dunfermline*

On 20 June 1605, the painter in St Giles' was paid 40 shillings 'to green My Lady Chancellor's seat', in keeping with the church's interior colour scheme of white-washed walls and green pillars.[1] The Lord Chancellor was now Alexander Seton, 1st Earl of Dunfermline, whose first marriage had vividly demonstrated the interplay between politics and religion in post-Reformation Scotland. Lilias Drummond (3) had died on 8 May 1601, and in the autumn of that same year her forty-six-year-old widower married Grizel Leslie, another Protestant teenager.[2]

What was the reason for this unseemly haste? Seton was not looking for a handsome dowry, for he was already a very wealthy man. There were other, more pressing considerations. Four of his and Lilias's five daughters had survived, but he had no male heir to succeed him, and that was a major problem.[3] He was determined to have a son to inherit his extensive estates. Apart from the fact that his four small daughters were now motherless, another concern was that James VI had given his infant son Prince Charles (the future Charles I) into the care of Seton and his wife. Looking after the Prince was, of course, a burden as well as a privilege, especially in this instance, because little Charles was very delicate.

However, Seton would have been well aware that it was only right that the child should be brought up in the household of a married couple. The danger was that with the death of Lilias, the royal infant might now be taken away and given to some other guardian, thereby depriving Seton of possible further favours from the grateful monarch.[4] In his search for a new wife, his thoughts turned to Lilias's relatives. Her sisters were not available, for Catherine and Jean Drummond were both married already. However, Catherine was the second wife of James Leslie, Master of Rothes and step-mother to his children. Grizel, her youngest step-daughter, had only been about nine when her mother died.[5] Now she was of marriageable age, healthy and presentable.

As Seton's wife she should have a glittering future. Both her father and the Drummond family would have known him well, as indeed Grizel probably did, and he no doubt assured them that he would respect her religious affiliation and be a kind husband to her. Contemporaries and later historians alike have agreed that he was not only highly intelligent but modest, had strong aesthetic interests and possessed a nicely self-deprecating sense of humour.[6] (Plate 2) Their marriage contract was duly signed on 27 October 1601, and Grizel would bring with her a handsome tocher of 30,000 merks, payable in three instalments.[7]

Prince Charles stayed where he was and the satisfied King conferred upon Seton the earldom of Dunfermline and made him Lord Chancellor of Scotland in 1602. The following year James VI inherited the throne of England, moved to London and in 1604 Dunfermline personally took the little Prince south to join the rest of the royal family. Meanwhile, Grizel's first child, apparently born in November 1602, was a daughter whom they named Lilias, after Dunfermline's first wife.[8] Her arrival was disappointing, of course, but in 1604 Grizel gave birth to the much desired son. He was baptised Charles, only to die the following year, reputedly of the plague. In 1606 a second daughter was born and was called Jean, probably after Lilias's sister.[9]

There would be no more children, however, for Grizel died on 6 September of that year. She did not leave a personal Will, but her Testament records the fact that her moveable goods and the debts owed to her came to more than £23,000 Scots, a very substantial sum.[10] She was buried beside her predecessor Lilias, in the vault at St Bridget's Church, Dalgety. Dunfermline would go on to marry for a third time, but it is intriguing to note that when he himself died in 1622 he left in the wardrobe of his house of Pinkie a coffer containing seven skirts with elaborately embroidered trains of satin and cloth of tissue. In Scotland, as elsewhere, there were at that period strict rules about what different sections of society might wear, and only women of the upper aristocracy were allowed to appear in skirts with trains, emphasising their status.[11] These at Pinkie, his testamentary inventory explains, had belonged to 'the said late noble Earl's first two ladies'.[12]

---

[1] ECA, MS Dean of Guild Accounts 1568-1626, n/p, 20 June 1605

[2] *Scots Peerage*, vii, 47; George Seton, *Memoir of Alexander Seton, Earl of Dunfermline* (Edinburgh 1882), 150-51; *The Historie of the House of Seytoun to the Year MDLIX by Sir Richard Maitland of Lethington With the Continuation by Alexander, Viscount Kingston to MDVII*, (Glasgow 1829), 63-64; Maurice Lee Jr, 'King James's Popish Chancellor' in *The Renaissance and Reformation in Scotland*, ed. Ian B. Cowan and Duncan Shaw (Scottish Academic Press 1983), 170-173

[3] NRS, Wills and Testaments, Edinburgh Commissary Court, CC8/8/44/635-637 (Lilias Drummond)

[4] *Scots Peerage*, iii, 370; Ethel Carleton Williams, *Anne of Denmark* (London 1970), 97-8

[5] Ibid., vii, 47-48

[6] Lee, 'King James's Popish Chancellor', 175-181

[7] K.H. Leslie, *Historical Records of the Family of Leslie from 1067 to 1868-9*, ii (Edinburgh 1869), 91

[8] According to Seton, op. cit., Lilias was baptised in November 1602, but the baptism does not appear to be recorded anywhere in NRS, Old Parish Registers

[9] *Scots Peerage, iii, 373;* Seton, op. cit., 151-153; *Bruce Gordon Seton, The House of Seton: A Study of Lost Causes* (Edinburgh 1939), 305-306

[10] NRS, Wills and Testaments, Edinburgh Commissary Court, CC8/8/45/7-11 (Grizel Leslie)

[11] Frances J. Shaw, 'Sumptuary Legislation in Scotland' in *The Juridical Review: The Law Journal of Scottish Universities* (Edinburgh 1979), Part 2, 81-112

[12] NRS, Wills and Testaments, Edinburgh Commissary Court, CC8/8/53/241-256 (Alexander Seton, 1st Earl of Dunfermline)

# 5

## *Helen Somerville, Lady Skene*

Helen Somerville was the eldest daughter of Sir John Somerville of Cambusnethan and his second wife Catherine Murray who was, according to the family historian, famous not only for her breeding, her beauty and her eloquence but also for her persistent attempts to have her stepson disinherited in favour of her own eight children.[1] In this somewhat troubled atmosphere, Helen and her siblings were brought up at Cambusnethan House, in the Upper Clyde Valley and in 1577 she was married to a successful lawyer with a cosmopolitan background. He was John Skene of Curriehill.

Born about 1540, he was a graduate of Aberdeen University, and had later spent seven years studying law in Paris and visiting Switzerland, Poland and Scandinavia. He had then settled at the University of Wittenberg in Germany, emerging as a fluent speaker of German. His friend Sir James Melville assured King James VI that he could also make 'long harangues in Latin', which of course was at that time regarded as being a universal language. In 1574 he finally returned to Scotland to take up a career as an advocate.[2] His years abroad no doubt explain why, in his middle or late thirties, he was still unmarried.

Quite how Helen and he came together is unknown, but they must have spent their married life in Edinburgh while Skene's career progressed. He became Clerk Register and a Lord of Session thanks, it was said, to the influence of Lord Blantyre, who was married to one of Helen's sisters. The author of the first published dictionary of Scots Law, Skene was knighted by 1604 and purchased Curriehill in Balerno, just outside Edinburgh. Meanwhile, Helen brought up their four sons and four daughters: James, who married Janet Johnston **(29)**, John, Alexander and William, at least two of whom became advocates, and Jane, Margaret, Catherine and Euphemia.[3] She was given her own seat in St Giles' in November 1608, featuring as 'The Lady Register'.[4] By then her husband was nearing the completion of his ten years' work on *Regiam Majestatem*, a major collection of Scottish legal statues dating back to the Middle Ages. It was published in both English and in Latin in 1609,[5] the Latin version being undertaken so that it could be read and understood by continental lawyers. He had the monopoly of printing these volumes, which brought him great fame and a considerable amount of money.

Skene died on 16 March 1617, aged about seventy-seven. His Will, composed five years earlier, gives us a glimpse of his relationship with Helen and shows that she must have had a hand in the business side of *Regiam Majestatem*. After a fairly lengthy introduction referring to the joy and heavenly pleasure prepared for Christ's 'elect and chosen folk, whereof I am assured to be one, through true and lively faith in the blood of Jesus Christ', he went on to nominate her as his only executor, having had, he said, long and good experience of her faithfulness and honesty, 'her dexterity in ruling mine and her affairs' and the motherly love she had towards her bairns. She was to deal with all his goods and gear, the copies of both the Latin and English editions of *Regiam Majestatem* which happened to be in his possession when he died, the rights he had over publication of that work, and all the books he had in his library at the time of his death.[6] He was buried in Greyfriars Church, the fragments of his stone later removed, with others, to the graveyard.[7] Helen registered his Will on 8 July 1617.[8] Her own date of death has not been recorded.

---

[1] James, 11th Lord Somerville, *Memorie* [sic] *of the Somervilles, being a History of the Baronial House of Somerville* (Edinburgh 1815), i, 425-441

[2] *Memorials of the family of Skene of Skene*, ed. W. F. Skene (New Spalding Club 1887), i, 107-8; Athol Murray, 'Skene, Sir John of Curriehill', *ODNB* (Oxford University Press 2004)

[3] Skene, op. cit., 111-112

[4] ECA, MS Dean of Guild Accounts 1568-1626, 1608 n/p, 1615, 16

[5] Skene, op. cit., 109-111; Murray, op. cit; Scot of Scotstarvet, 99; Brunton, *Lords of Session*, 230

[6] NRS, Wills and Testaments, Edinburgh Commissary Court CC8/8/49/620-622 (Sir John Skene)

[7] NRS, Wills and Testaments, Edinburgh Commissary Court CC8/8/56/384-386 (Sir James Skene), referring to his father's tomb; Anonymous, *The Most Famous Epitaphs and Monumental Inscriptions in the Greyfriars Churchyard, Edinburgh, etc* (British Library 1893), 53-4

[8] NRS, Wills and Testaments, Edinburgh Commissary Court CC8/8/49/620 (Sir John Skene)

# 6

## *Margaret Collace, Lady Preston*

Margaret Collace received her seat in St Giles' fairly late on in her career, when she was about to marry her third husband. The names of her parents are not known, but she came from the Collace family who were proprietors of Balnamoon, near Brechin in Angus.[1] She had first of all married Walter Reid, former Abbot of Kinloss, which was one of the richest Cistercian abbeys in Scotland. Of course Roman Catholic ecclesiastics were not allowed to marry but with the coming of the Reformation Reid had been revealed as one of its enthusiastic supporters, sitting in the 1560 parliament which forbade the celebration of Mass and the following February approving of the Act which sanctioned the marriage of churchmen. His monks also conformed.

He was then granted the title of Commendator of Kinloss, meaning that he could retain and administer the former Abbey buildings and lands for life, but he disposed of most of the lands and in 1572 resigned from the position of Commendator.[2] Perhaps that was about the time when Margaret became his wife. They went on to have four children: three daughters, Isobel, Christian (the seventeenth-century version of Christina) and Anna, and then a son, James. They seem to have spent most of their time in the north, living modestly at Kinloss, possibly in part of the former Abbey, with Reid also farming Muirton, near Forres in Moray, which he had settled on Margaret. They had a surprisingly large number of servants. Perhaps some of these were the former monks.

Reid died in Edinburgh on 17 December 1588 and, as listed in his Testament, his household had included John Young the gardener and Mr Alexander Spittell, schoolmaster, who was paid £24 a year for teaching 'the said late Abbot's bairns.' That would imply that the children were all still minors when he died, which would fit in with their parents having married in about 1572. Strange as it may seem to us, Reid had continued to be known as 'the Abbot of Kinloss' for the rest of his life, no doubt colloquially but also in some official documents as well and that is how he is termed in his Testament. Margaret, who registered it, was described as 'Lady Kinloss', but in later years and despite her other marriages she features as 'Lady Muirton'. The Testament notes that Reid left £773:13:4 after his debts had been paid, so he had not accumulated enormous wealth.[3]

Margaret handed in the Testament to be registered on 27 March 1591, and in that same year she married Sir John Shairp of Houston, a widower who had ten children by his two previous wives, his second wife having been a cousin of Walter Reid. Shairp was an advocate, a very successful and prominent figure who had been involved in money-lending, like many of his colleagues, and had purchased a great deal of property including the estate of Houston near Linlithgow, where he would begin the construction of a tower house in about 1600. It survives to this day.[4]

His career meant that he spent much time in Edinburgh, but in 1603 we have a glimpse of Margaret at Houston while he was in town. She had a liferent of the Mains of Houston, by her marriage contract, and in April that year construction work was evidently still going on at Houston House, for she was anxiously consulting her husband's secretary about how much she should give in drink silver

[tips] to the masons who were constantly demanding them, while the cook was complaining that the kitchen chimney was using up far too much fuel. She was not usually out of her depth when supervising the household at Houston, however, and a month later, when one of Shairp's employees was checking up on which tenants had given in their rents for the previous year, he found that Margaret knew exactly who had complied.[5]

On 17 October 1607 Shairp died an extremely wealthy man who left not only his various properties but almost £58,000 once his debts were paid. Thirteen days earlier, he had made his Will, 'tied to his bed at the pleasure of God by an infirmity and disease'. His greatest concern in doing so was to prevent any discord that might arise between his 'beloved spouse', his children and relatives after his death, a sentiment which he repeated towards the end of his Will. This might suggest that Margaret had not always got on with her stepchildren, but equally it could simply have been the preoccupation of a judge who had seen all too many quarrels about bequests. He was not the only lawyer to express a similar wish. Two of his sons were to be his executors, with the advice of Margaret, and his granddaughter Agnes Shairp, whose father was dead, was told to remain with Margaret until her marriage.[6]

Margaret herself remarried in 1609. Her third husband was the eminent judge, John Preston, Lord Fentonbarns. He too had been married twice before,[7] and Margaret had known him for a long time. When she had gone to register her first husband's Testament in 1591, Preston had been in charge of the Commissary Court of Edinburgh, and he had signed the note of its registration.[8] In 1596, he had become a Senator of the College of Justice as Lord Fentonbarns, and now his career had taken a leap forward. Since the end of

1607 he had been acting as Vice-President of the Court of Justice, in the absence of the then President, Lord Balmerino, who had fallen from royal favour. On 10 March 1609 Balmerino, a Roman Catholic, was tried for treason, having engaged in correspondence with Pope Clement VIII. This brought with it the death sentence, and everyone knew that Fentonbarns would succeed him.[9] Fentonbarns apparently decided that he would need a wife in his new and prestigious position. Very early that year he married Margaret, and in February £5 was paid for timber for her seat in St Giles'.[10] In the end, Balmerino's conviction for treason was set aside and he was allowed to live out his life in retirement. Fentonbarns replaced him formally as Lord President on 6 June 1609.

Margaret and he would have lived in his handsome house in Blackfriars Wynd with its elaborately carved wooden façade, and would presumably have been regular attenders at St Giles'. He remained as Lord President until his death on 14 June 1616.[11] Margaret died on 25 September 1617, having signed her Testament five days earlier with her hand held at the pen, 'because I cannot write in respect of my disease'. Sir James Reid, her son by her first husband, was her executor and her name is given as 'Lady Muirton'.[12]

---

[1] *The Charters of the Priory of Beauly* ed. E.C. Batten (Grampian Club, 1877), 232

[2] *The Heads of Religious Houses in Scotland from Twelfth to Sixteenth Centuries*, edd. D. E. R. Watt and N. F. Shead (Scottish Record Society 2001), 17-18; *The Charters of the Priory of Beauly*, 232

[3] NRS, Wills and Testaments, Edinburgh Commissary Court, CC8/8/23/174-177 (Walter Reid)

[4] Margaret H. B. Sanderson, 'Shairp, Sir John, of Houston', *ODNB* (Oxford University Press 2004); Margaret H. B. Sanderson, *Mary Stewart's People* (Edinburgh 1987), 27, 29, 30

[5] Sanderson, *Mary Stewart's People*, 29, 30

[6] NRS, Wills and Testaments, Edinburgh Commissary Court, CC8/8/44/46-58 (Sir John Shairp)

[7] Athol Murray, 'Preston, John, of Penicuik, Lord Fentonbarns', *ODNB* (Oxford University Press 2004)

[8] NRS, Wills and Testaments, Edinburgh Commissary Court, CC8/8/23/174-177 (Walter Reid)

[9] R.R. Zulager, 'Elphinstone, James, first Lord Balmerino,' *ODNB* (Oxford University Press 2004); William Fraser, *The Elphinstone Family Book of the Lords Elphinstone, Balmerino and Couper*, ii (Edinburgh 1897), 177, 178; Brunton, *Lords of Session*, 313-317

[10] ECA, MS Dean of Guild Accounts, 1568-1626, February 1609, n/p

[11] Robert Chambers, *Traditions of Edinburgh*, (Edinburgh 1825), i, 97; Athol Murray, 'Preston, John, of Penicuik, Lord Fentonbarns', *ODNB* (Oxford University Press 2004)

[12] NRS, Wills and Testaments, Edinburgh Commissary Court, CC8/8/58/298-9 (Margaret Collace)

# 7

## *Elizabeth Heriot, Lady Torphichen*

In 1610, the Edinburgh Dean of Guild paid £5:6:8 for timber for a seat for Lady Torphichen in St Giles', for the making of it, and a further 6 shillings and 8 pence for its lock.[1] Elizabeth Heriot was by then the mother of six children, ranging from James, aged about fourteen, through John, William, Robert and Isabel to Henry, aged five. If they accompanied her to church, they would probably have been sent to sit on the forms reserved for offspring of the congregation, the notion being that, by grouping children together near the pulpit under the watchful eye of the minister, they would be prevented from running about and disturbing the service, a perennial problem.[2]

Elizabeth was the daughter of James Heriot, Laird of Trabroun in the parish of Gladsmuir, East Lothian. A cousin of Thomas, 1st Earl of Haddington, her father was also related to George Heriot, the royal jeweller, and the family proudly recalled that George Buchanan, the famous Reformer, had been the grandson of a previous Laird.[3] Elizabeth herself had impressive connections through her mother, Isabel Maitland, the highly educated daughter of the poet Sir Richard Maitland of Lethington, one of her uncles being Lord Chancellor Thirlestane, husband of Jean Fleming **(1)**.

Elizabeth would have been twenty or so when her marriage contract with James Sandilands, Baron of Calder, was signed on 1 August 1595. He was about the same age and earlier that year he had been in trouble for taking part in a riot in Edinburgh between the Sandilands family and supporters of the 3ʳᵈ Earl of Montrose (grandfather of the famous Marquis of Montrose). However, his prospects were good, for he was heir to his great-uncle, the 1ˢᵗ Lord Torphichen. The latter had been Preceptor of Torphichen Priory before the Reformation, and afterwards Mary, Queen of Scots had in 1564 created a temporal lordship for him, giving him possession of the Priory properties.[4]

Elizabeth's wedding would have taken place shortly after the signing of her marriage contract, and two years later she became Lady Torphichen when her husband duly inherited the title of Lord Torphichen from his great-uncle. He did not play any major role in public life, but occupied himself with selling off many of the Torphichen Priory lands.[5] Their youngest son Thomas, was baptised on 21 June 1612, and Elizabeth must have died soon afterwards, or perhaps in childbirth, for she disappears from the records and Torphichen remarried. He had no children with his second wife, and died in 1617.[6]

It would be interesting to know how much influence her mother Isabel Maitland had on Elizabeth and indeed on Elizabeth's children, encouraging them, perhaps, in the Maitland family's literary tradition. When she made her Will in 1618, at 'a great age' and as 'a faithful Christian', Isabel unusually included her books. Few of her female contemporaries had enough books to merit such a mention, but Isabel did, bequeathing 'all her French books' to her great nephew the Viscount [later 1ˢᵗ Earl] of Lauderdale. The rest she left to Elizabeth's son William. Isabel died in 1621.[7]

---

[1] ECA, MS Dean of Guild Accounts 1568-1626, 1610, n/p

[2] *Scots Peerage*, viii, 390-391; Harry Bertram McCall, *The History and Antiquities of the parish of Mid-Calder* (Edinburgh 1894), 76

[3] George Willis Ballingall, *Collections and Notes Historical and Genealogical regarding the Heriots of Trabroun, Scotland* (Edinburgh, 1878), 19-21, 29; *A Biographical History of Eminent Scotsmen*, ed. Robert Chambers, iii (Glasgow 1835), 42

[4] *Scots Peerage*, viii, 387

[5] Ibid., 390

[6] Ibid., 390-391

[7] NRS, Wills and Testaments, Edinburgh Commissary Court, CC8/8/51/472-476 (Isabel Maitland)

# 8

## *Agnes Lindsay, Lady Tungland*

Agnes Lindsay was another of those women whose choice of a second husband brought her an enhanced position in society. The names of her parents are unknown, but she makes her first appearance in the records in March 1582, as the wife of James Murray of Pardewis, near Dunfermline.[1] She had probably been born in the 1560s and would have been about twenty years younger than he was. A widower at the time of their marriage, he came from a Perthshire family, being the third son of Sir William Murray of Tullibardine, but his interests had soon focused on Edinburgh during the reign of Mary, Queen of Scots. He had on two occasions fixed placards to the door of the Tolbooth next to St Giles', vehemently accusing the Earl of Bothwell and his associates of murdering the Queen's husband, Lord Darnley. His first wife had been Marion Preston, the daughter of Edinburgh's Lord Provost.

By the time that Agnes and he married, Murray was Master of the King's Wardrobe and was accumulating various other properties in Fife, but their country home seems to have remained at Pardewis. He obviously had to spend a good deal of time at Court, and he was soon in trouble. He supported the Protestant Ruthven Raiders, who in 1582 captured James VI and held him prisoner for ten months in order to end the King's patronage of the Roman Catholic Duke of Lennox.[2] Agnes was pregnant by then. Her son John was baptised on 27 January 1583 in the Church of the Holy Trinity, now known as Dunfermline

Abbey.[3] When the King regained his freedom, Murray was forfeited, losing his lands. That was in 1584. He and Agnes would have had to move out of Pardewis, although the estate does not seem to have been given to anyone else, and the following year his properties were restored to him after the Raiders gained control once more. Agnes's second son, Patrick, was baptised in the Church of the Holy Trinity on 9 October 1586.[4] They also had a daughter Jean, at some unspecified date and place.[5]

After that, their life seems to have settled down again, but James Murray lived for only a further six years, dying on 28 September 1592. He was buried in the Dunfermline parish churchyard, where his surviving tombstone bears his coat of arms, displaying three stars within an ornamental border, his name and the exact date of his death.[6] His Testament lists his goods and financial obligations. These were in keeping with the lifestyle of a country laird and his wife. Their household furnishings, his clothing, the silverwork and other belongings were estimated to be worth £133, his total moveables with the addition of debts owed to him amounting to a fairly meagre £522. His three young children were named as his executors, and the Testament was handed in for registration on 29 July 1594 by Agnes, 'his relict spouse, now spouse to William Melville, Commendator of Tungland'.[7]

Agnes's second marriage brought her considerably improved status. Her new husband's title meant that he owned the property of the pre-Reformation monks of Tungland Abbey in Galloway and he also acquired the lands of Kilwinning Abbey in Ayrshire. His own family background, however, was in Fife, for he was a younger son of Sir John Melville of Raith, near Kirkcaldy, and this may explain how he came to marry Agnes, if she was from the Dunfermline area. According to his brother, the famous Sir James Melville of Halhill, Tungland was 'a good scholar' who spoke perfect Latin, Dutch, Flemish and French.

He had spent some time in the Netherlands in the service of the Prince of Orange and he was often involved in diplomatic business. He made preparations, for instance, for the arrival of Anne of Denmark in Scotland for her marriage to James VI, and for the entertainment of foreign ambassadors at the baptism of their first son, Prince Henry Frederick.[8] Apart from these activities Melville had become a Lord of Session in 1587, was frequently one of the commissioners for opening the Scottish parliament in the early 1600s and in 1607 was a member of the Privy Council.[9] Three years later, Agnes was granted her seat in St Giles'.[10]

By this time she had a son and possibly two daughters with Tungland. The son was named Frederick, a unique first name in Scotland in those days, and no doubt chosen in honour of Anne of Denmark's father, King Frederick II. Their daughter Sophia, born in 1599,[11] does not seem to have survived and another daughter, named after herself, died young.[12] Lord Tungland himself died on 3 October 1613, after an illness during which he was treated with 'drugs and medicaments' by Thomas Adamson, apothecary and James Skinner, surgeon. He had nominated Frederick as his only executor, and his Testament gives us a glimpse of his and Agnes's domestic life. Surprisingly, only three items of silver were listed: a silver spoon, a silver coin and a silver salt. These were valued at £60 Scots, but Tungland's library was estimated to be worth £200 and the combined total of his inventory and the debts owed to him came to a very handsome £10,720, while he owed only £434.[13] Their son Frederick died in March 1614, his

Testament revealing that he had inherited the silver spoon, the silver coin and the silver salt, along with half of his father's library as well, of course, as his lands.[14] There is no record of the death of Agnes, but the wording of her husband's Testament indicates that she had predeceased him.

---

[1] NRS, Papers of the Henderson Family of Fordell, GD172/134/1

[2] *Scots Peerage,* i, 461-463; J.R.M. Sizer, 'Murray, James, of Pardewis', *ODNB* (Oxford University Press 2004)

[3] *Parish Registers of Dunfermline 1561-1700,* ed. Henry Paton (Scottish Record Society 1911), 70

[4] *Scots Peerage,* i, 461-463; *Parish Registers of Dunfermline,* 83

[5] NRS, Wills and Testaments, Edinburgh Commissary Court, CC8/8/26/698-700 (James Murray of Pardewis)

[6] Peter Chalmers, *Historical and Statistical Account of Dunfermline,* i, (Edinburgh 1859), 422

[7] NRS, Wills and Testaments, Edinburgh Commissary Court, CC8/8/26/698-700 (James Murray of Pardewis)

[8] Fraser, *The Melvilles,* 171

[9] Brunton, *Lords of Session,* 214-215; *Scots Peerage,* vi, 94-95

[10] ECA, MS Dean of Guild Accounts 1568-1626, n/p 1610

[11] *Scots Peerage,* vi, 95; *Parish Registers of Dunfermline,* 104

[12] Fraser, *The Melvilles,* 171

[13] NRS, Wills and Testaments, Edinburgh Commissary Court, CC8/8/47, 655-658 (William Melville)

[14] NRS, Wills and Testaments, Edinburgh Commissary Court, CC8/8/48/131-132 (Frederick Melville)

# 9

## *Nichola Somerville, Lady Blantyre*

Nichola Somerville, sister of Helen Somerville (5), was the youngest daughter of Sir John Somerville and his wife, Catherine Murray. She was brought up in the family home, Cambusnethan House in the upper Clyde Valley, and like Helen, she made an important marriage. In April 1582 she became the wife of Walter Stewart, Commendator of Blantyre. He and King James VI had been brought up together, taught by the famous Reformer George Buchanan. He remained a close friend of the King, who by the time Stewart married had conferred upon him the lands of the Priory of Blantyre, dissolved at the Reformation. Despite a quarrel with James VI, which led to him being briefly imprisoned in Edinburgh Castle in 1599, Stewart's career flourished. He was a Lord of Session, was made Lord High Treasurer of Scotland in 1596, became a member of the Privy Council, and in 1606 was created Lord Blantyre.[1] According to one of Sir John Scot of Scotstarvet's idiosyncratic anecdotes, as Blantyre rode up Edinburgh High Street on one occasion, he fell from his horse and broke his leg, whereupon a courtier joked that it was not surprising that the horse could not bear his weight, for ' he had so many offices engrossed in his person.'[2]

He and Nichola had their principal country home at Cardonald Place, the medieval castle which his father had acquired in the parish of Paisley. It was demolished in the nineteenth century and a farm now stands on the site. From time to time they also used the old Priory of Blantyre which had 'a fruitful orchard' and was known as Blantyre Craig, after the large rock upon which it had been built. It stood on the left bank of the River Clyde, not far from Bothwell on the opposite bank. The rest of their time was spent in Edinburgh.[3] It was in 1610, when her husband had been appointed to the newly reconstructed Privy Council, that Nichola joined her sister Helen in having her own seat in St Giles', one of those made 'at the Council's command'.[4]

The previous year, she had suffered a painful tragedy. She and her husband had four sons and two daughters: James, William, Walter, a doctor of medicine, John, a graduate, Anna and Joan.[5] James, her eldest son, was killed on 8 November 1609. An accomplished young man and the godson of King James VI and I, he had gone to live at the Court in London and married a daughter of the 4th Earl of Huntingdon. Not long afterwards he quarrelled with Sir George Wharton while they were gaming. As a lengthy ballad of the time describes, they fought a duel in Islington, at that time a village a mile outside London. Equipped with rapiers and daggers and in their shirtsleeves to show that they wore no hidden armour, both men were fatally wounded and died in each other's arms. They were buried together in the same grave in St Mary's Churchyard, Islington, on the orders of the King.[6] Blantyre, James's 'aged father', was described as being 'so far overcome with anguish, grief and sorrow that he is altogether insensible' and could do no business.[7] Nichola must have been equally distraught.

Her husband made his Will at Cardonald on 24 February 1617, signing it with his own hand, and making Nichola his sole executor. He died shortly afterwards. The value of his goods, which included the usual crops and cattle, an old brown horse, a silver basin and laver, 3 silver cups, a salt and 5 spoons, along with debts owed to him, came to a handsome £7832. The debts he owed to other people amounted to £1340. For the rest of her life, Nichola was to have the use of all the furnishings at Dundonald Place, provided she did not remove or alter any of them, for when she died her second son William, now the heir, would inherit them. The same was to apply to Blantyre Craig.

After some lengthy religious reflections suggestive of genuine devotion, Blantyre ordered William to be 'thankful and kind' to his mother and his siblings, 'and to aid them and assist them in all their honest actions.' The Earl of Mar and three other friends were to help Nichola, and if any controversy were to arise between her and her children, or between any of the siblings, then these friends should intervene and settle the disagreements. If they did not do so, Blantyre said sternly, they would deserve his curse rather than his blessing. Nichola must also take their advice in everything concerning his Testament and the payment of his debts and bequests. Among the four witnesses to the Testament was George Hutcheson, the successful notary and banker who founded Hutcheson's Hospital in Glasgow. Nichola duly handed in the Testament for registration at Glasgow Commissary Court on 12 June 1618. Her own date of death is unknown.[8]

---

[1]*Scots Peerage*, ii, 81-83; Zulager, R. 'Stewart, Walter, first Lord Blantyre', *ODNB* (Oxford University Press 2004); Brunton, *Lords of Session*, 225-226

[2] Scot of Scotstarvet, 55-56

[3] NRS, Wills and Testaments, Glasgow Commissary Court CC9/7/15/66, 68 (Walter Stewart, 1st Lord Blantyre); Historic Environment Scotland, Canmore ID 44383; J.R.N. Macphail, 'The Haunting of Blantyre Craig' in *Scottish Historical Review*, xv, no. 59 (April 1918), 201; William Hamilton of Wishaw, *Descriptions of the*

*Sheriffdoms of Lanark and Renfrew compiled about MDCCX,* (Glasgow 1831), 15

[4] E.C.A., MS Dean of Guild Accounts 1568-1626, 1608 n/p

[5] *Scots Peerage,* ii, 81-85

[6] Samuel Lewis Jr, *The History and Topography of the parish of St Mary Islington* (London 1842), 244-47; Scot of Scotstarvet, 56; S. Allen Chambers Jr, *History of St Mary Islington* (London 2017), 14-15

[7] *Scots Peerage,* ii, 84

[8] NRS, Wills and Testaments, Glasgow Commissary Court CC9/7/15/66, 68 (Walter Stewart, 1st Lord Blantyre)

# 10

## *Elizabeth Hay, Lady Whitburgh*

Did the members of the St Giles' congregation who saw Elizabeth Hay sitting in her own seat there recall that her grandfather had been James Hay, the pre-Reformation Bishop of Ross, and that her father Thomas was one of his illegitimate sons?[1] Thomas has often been referred to as 'the last Abbot of Glenluce', but he was not quite that. In the spring of 1560 the Pope had appointed him to be Commendator of Glenluce, a minor Cistercian abbey in Dumfries and Galloway. That did not necessarily imply that he too was a churchman, although it is likely that he was. At any rate, it did mean that he would have taken on the functions of the abbot.

With the coming of the Reformation a few months later, he and the monks conformed to Protestantism and his position as Commendator was renewed. He would have had no spiritual role, but possessed and administered the Abbey buildings and lands for the rest of his life.[2] He was also now free to marry. Isabel Kennedy, no doubt a relative of his patron Gilbert Kennedy, 4th Earl of Cassillis,[3] became his wife and their daughter Elizabeth would have been brought up at Glenluce, where her father was based.

Elizabeth might have been expected to marry someone from the west of Scotland but instead her husband was an Edinburgh man, Alexander Hay, possibly a relative of the Earls of Errol. At any rate, he was an eligible partner. A younger son of Alexander Hay, the eminent Lord Clerk Register and Court of Session judge who was known by his legal title of Lord Easter Kennet,[4] Hay had been to school in Musselburgh, graduated from university, and spent the rest of his career diligently working in the capital and frequently travelling to James VI's Court in London. He and Elizabeth probably married during his early years as clerk to the Privy Council and the Court of Session.

The date of their wedding is unrecorded, but they went on to have four surviving children: George, Francis, Jean and William.[5] Despite Sir John Scot of Scotstarvet's characteristically dismissive remark that Hay was 'not learned,' his career prospered. He became Secretary of State for Scotland in 1608 and two years later he was made a Lord of Session, with the title of Lord Newton.[6] It was during 1610-1611 that the wright in St Giles' was paid £1:6/- for making Elizabeth's seat.[7] For some reason Lord Newton later changed his title to Lord Whitburgh and in 1612 he succeeded his father as Lord Clerk Register.[8]

Elizabeth and he lived in comfortable circumstances. When he died in 1616, the inventory of his goods records a fine collection of silver, no doubt used to impress when entertaining. Much of it silver gilt, there were basins with matching ewers, cups, bowls, salts and spoons. What was obviously their main chamber was hung with nine pieces of tapestry worth £348, extending to 116 ells (an ell measured 37 inches) while another room had 7 ells of green figured velvet. Lord Whitburgh's Testament shows too that he employed six men servants, including a steward, and three women servants. In all, his goods, not counting the debts that he owed, came to just short of £5000. Elizabeth, however, had not enjoyed her special St Giles' seat for long. Her date of death is unknown, but in a charter of February 1615 she is termed 'the late Dame Elizabeth Hay'.[9]

[1] *The Heads of Religious Houses in Scotland from Twelfth to Sixteenth Centuries* edited by D. E .R. Watt and N. F. Shead (Scottish Record Society 2001), 66; Charles H. Haws, *Scottish Parish Clergy at the Reformation 1540-1574* (Scottish Record Society 1972), 167, 223

[2] Mark Dilworth, 'The Commendator System in Scotland' in *The Innes Review*, xxxvii, no. 2 (Glasgow 1986), 51-72; James Kirk, *Patterns of Reform: Continuity and Change in the Reformation Kirk* (Edinburgh 1989), 179; *The Books of Assumption of the Thirds of Benefices,* ed. James Kirk (The British Academy 1995), lii-liii, 600; John Dowden, *Bishops of Scotland*, ed. J. Maitland Thomson (Glasgow 1912), 221-222

[3] Cistercian Abbey: Glenluce: https://www.dhi.ac.uk/cistercians/abbeys/glenluce.php

[4] R.R. Zulager, 'Hay, Alexander, of Easter Kennet, Lord Easter Kennet', *ODNB* (Oxford University Press 2004); *Scot of Scotstarvet*, 100

[5] NRS, Wills and Testaments, Edinburgh Commissary Court, CC8/8/49, 592 (Alexander Hay)

[6] Brunton, *Lords of Session*, 252

[7] ECA, MS Dean of Guild Accounts 1568-1626, 1610-1611 n/p

[8] Zulager, 'Hay, Alexander'; *Handbook of British Chronology*, 190; Brunton, *Lords of Session*, 252

[9] *The Records of the Parliaments of Scotland to 1707*, edd. K.M. Brown *et al* (St Andrews 2007-18), http://www.rps.ac.uk

# 11

## *Helen Arnot, Lady Home*

Helen Arnot was one of the daughters of Sir John Arnot of Berswick, Provost of Edinburgh from 1608 until his death in 1616, and his second wife Margaret Craig.[1] He belonged to the elite group of merchants who made their fortunes in foreign trade and were highly influential in the affairs of the capital. When Helen married on 11 May 1595, not only was her father extremely wealthy but her bridegroom Isaac Morrison was the son of another prosperous Edinburgh merchant family.[2] Himself a merchant burgess of Edinburgh, Isaac made a fortune and took a leading part in the town's administration, becoming a bailie.[3] Helen brought a large tocher with her, her father gave her additional property, and she and her husband lived in very comfortable circumstances.

Their marriage lasted until 27 February 1610, when Isaac died, leaving Helen with five young children under the age of 15: Harry, James, Margaret, Katherine and Agnes.[4] He was buried in Greyfriars Churchyard, Edinburgh, beside his father, because the St Giles' churchyard had become so overcrowded with the passage of time that in 1561 the town closed it, decreeing that burials must in future take place at Greyfriars, less than five minutes' walk away. An exception was made only occasionally, seemingly in the case of John Knox himself, for instance.

According to the Latin epitaph on Isaac's memorial, both he and his father were 'rich in wealth and honour of the Town.'[5] That was certainly true, for Isaac left over £63,000 listed in the inventory of his moveables and the enormous total of debts owing to him.[6] Despite the responsibilities of her young family, Helen now became that sought after figure in the marriage market, a wealthy widow, and a suitor was quick to make his move. On 2 September of that same year, she became the wife of Sir George Home of Manderston, a widower with three teenage children[7] and within a year the Dean of Guild's accounts record the payment of £10 to the wright for making her seat in St Giles' and furnishing the wainscot for it.[8]

Sir George must have seemed to be a promising partner. He owned the estate of Manderston, just outside Duns in Berwickshire, but more to the point, he was the nephew of the influential George, 1st Earl of Dunbar who was pursuing a highly successful career at the Court in London.[9] Amongst his many offices and appointments, the Earl was a Knight of the Garter, a member of the Scottish Privy Council and Keeper of the Palace of Holyroodhouse. It was in the Kirk of Holyrood that Helen and Sir George had married. Significantly, the Earl had two daughters but no sons, and Sir George was generally regarded as being his heir. However, when the Earl died the following year, his title did not go to Sir George but became extinct.[10]

At first Helen's new marriage went well, and she had four more children: John, David, William and Anna.[11] Moreover Margaret, her eldest daughter from her first marriage, would later marry Alexander, Sir George's elder son from his first marriage.[12] So far so good, but ten years after their own wedding there was serious trouble between Helen and her husband. Her father was no longer alive to intervene, and when he had died in 1616 Sir George had been owing him the large sum of 14,000 merks.[13] He was still at Duns, but on 22 June 1620 Helen obtained a Decreet of Adherence against him, which means that he had left her at least four years earlier and was refusing to live with her.[14]

Worse was to follow. On 10 September 1628 Sir George arrived with three horsemen and four footmen, all English, and various others, armed with long staves, hagbuts (long-barrelled firearms) and pistols. They seized and carried off from what would have been Helen's jointure lands at Coldingham, eleven miles from Duns, 2 oxen, 20 sheep, 14 ewes, 22 young lambs and 9 cattle, in other words, all the livestock she possessed there, except her horse, 'which the said Sir George affirms he is sorry he missed.' He failed to appear in person before the Privy Council and was ordered to enter Edinburgh Tolbooth as a prisoner within six days.[15]

How long he remained there is unknown, but on 2 December 1628 the Privy Council heard a complaint submitted by Sir Thomas Hope, the Lord Advocate, on behalf of Helen, 'the unfortunate spouse of Sir George Home of Manderston'. Sir George, it said, had given her great grief, trouble and displeasure for several years past by persecuting her, being both unmindful and unthankful for the great estate provided with her by her late father, and being forgetful of his duty, first to God and then to her, his wife. He had reduced her to extreme misery and necessity, repudiated her from his company and allowed her nothing to live on until in the end she had in 1624 been forced to sue him before the Lords of Session. They had found in her favour, ordering her husband to pay her 1000 merks a year.[16]

Events soon took a distinctly sinister turn. The very next day, 3 December 1628, the Privy Council began to investigate allegations made by Alexander Hamilton, a notorious warlock who had been arrested and was now a prisoner in Edinburgh Tolbooth. He claimed that Helen had urged him to arrange her husband's death by means of witchcraft. Sir George and two possible witnesses were summoned by the Privy Council to come to Edinburgh and be examined as to what they knew. The witnesses failed to appear and Sir George declared that he could not possibly travel to Edinburgh without a safe conduct, for fear of being attacked by those who plotted his death. His excuse was accepted.

The two alleged witnesses, a couple of lawyers, were found and it emerged that in Duns Tolbooth they had copied out various depositions against Helen, in the presence of the local church ministers, who had then shown these to Hamilton the warlock in Edinburgh Tolbooth. He had confirmed them as being accurate accounts. Significantly he had also been visited by Sir George, who had obtained a safe conduct on the grounds that he needed to come to Edinburgh because Helen was pursuing an action for divorce against him. Appearing before the Lords of the Privy Council in person, he was now ordered to bring two of his own servants before them. By this time, it had been discovered that the various depositions contained many contradictions. Further investigations revealed that the charges against Helen had been devised only by Hamilton himself and the father of one of the lawyers involved.

By 2 February 1630, Alexander Hamilton had been condemned to death for witchcraft. Questioned by some of the Privy Council, he confessed that none of the accusations against Helen was true. Shortly afterwards, he was burned at the stake at Edinburgh Castle. Finally, on 17 June 1630, Sir George appeared once more before the Lords of the Privy Council and gave an obligation to the effect that in future he would in no way harm his wife, her servants and tenants, her goods or her gear, on pain of being fined £1000.[17] Helen's divorce was apparently granted, for when James Dalrymple, Viscount Stair, wrote his famous *Institutions of the Laws of Scotland* in 1693, he described how the innocent party in a divorce continued to enjoy the lands and possessions from the marriage just as if the person divorced was dead, while the offender lost all the previous benefits of the marriage. In so doing, Stair cited the case of Helen, Lady Manderston.[18]

Sir George's financial affairs seem to have gone from bad to worse after that, while Helen prospered.[19] By 1634-36 she was noted as having rented out a two-storey house in the Canongate. This had probably been one of her father's gifts to her, for she also had two cellars which were next to others owned by one of her sisters, Lady Prestongrange.[20] She was able to administer her jointure lands energetically without any interference from her troublesome former husband. She was, for instance, involved in a dispute with two of her tenants of Coldingham in 1638 over some teind sheaves. Her complaint was not upheld and instead she was told to cease troubling them about the matter.[21] In a document of 24 June 1643 she is referred to as the relict of Sir George Home of Manderston, so she outlived him.[22] She would have been in her sixties by then. She died before 20 October 1654, when their son Sir John Home was served heir to a tenement in Eyemouth which had belonged to her.[23]

---

[1] NRS, Wills and Testaments, Edinburgh Commissary Court, CC8/8/49/175-179 (Sir John Arnot)

[2] *Register of Marriages of the City of Edinburgh 1595-1700* ed. Henry Paton (Scottish Record Society 1905), 491

[3] NRS, Papers of the Brooke Family of Biel, GD6/938; *Roll of Edinburgh Burgesses and Guild Brethern, 1406-1700*, ed. Charles B. Boog Watson (Scottish Record Society 1929), 359

[4] NRS, Wills and Testaments, Edinburgh Commissary Court, CC8/8/46/439 (Isaac Morrison); NRS, GD6/938, Legal diligence at the instance of John Morrison, eldest son and heir of the deceased Isaac Morrison

[5] William Maitland, *History of Edinburgh from its Foundation to the Present Time, in 9 Books* (Edinburgh 1753), ii, 191

[6] NRS, Wills and Testaments, Edinburgh Commissary Court, CC8/8/46/439 (Isaac Morison)

[7] *Scots Peerage*, iii, 284; *Parish of Holyroodhouse or Canongate Register of Marriages 1564-1800* ed. Francis Grant (Scottish Record Society 1915), 632, where he is mistakenly called Alexander

[8] ECA, Dean of Guild MS Accounts 1568-1626, n/p 1610-1611

[9] *Scots Peerage*, iii, 286, 284

[10] Ibid., iii, 286-289; *Register of Marriages for the Parish of Edinburgh 1595-1700*, 453

[11] *Scots Peerage*, iii, 285

[12] Ibid., 284; *Register of the Great Seal, 1620-1633*, ed. J. Maitland Thomson (Edinburgh 1894), 51, number 153

[13] NRS, Wills and Testaments, Edinburgh Commissary Court, CC8/8/49/175-179 (Sir John Arnot)

[14] *Scots Peerage*, i, 72

[15] *Register of the Privy Council 1627-1628*, 2nd series, ii, ed. P. Hume Brown (Edinburgh 1900), 511-512

[16] Ibid.

[17] *Register of the Privy Council 1629-30*, 2nd series, iii, ed. P. Hume Brown (Edinburgh 1901), 361-362, 378, 389, 397, 400, 443, 560, 570, 582, 622; Julian Goodare, *The Scottish Witch-Hunt in Context* ed. Julian Goodare (Manchester 2002); *The Register of the Privy Council 1630-32*, 2nd series, iv, ed. P. Hume Brown (Edinburgh 1902), 55, 220

[18] James Dalrymple, Viscount Stair, *The Institutions of the Laws of Scotland* (Edinburgh 1693), cited in Andrew MacDowell, Lord Bankton, *An Institute of the Laws of Scotland in Civil Rights* (Edinburgh 1761), 140

[19] *Register of the Privy Council 1633-1635*, 2nd series, v, ed. P. Hume Brown (Edinburgh 1904), 241

[20] *Edinburgh Housemails Book*, 225, 226

[21] *Register of the Privy Council 1638-1643*, 2nd series, vii, ed. P. Hume Brown (Edinburgh 1906), 51, 54-55

[22] NRS, Papers of the family of Hume of Polwarth, Berwickshire, Earls of Marchmont, GD158/2809

[23] *Scots Peerage*, iii, 285

# 12

## *Isobel Seton, Countess of Lauderdale*

Lady Isobel Seton was born in 1593, the second of the five daughters of Alexander Seton, future Lord Chancellor of Scotland and his first wife, Lilias Drummond.[1] When Isobel was eight years old her mother died[2] and she and her sisters then had two successive young stepmothers, Grizel Leslie **(4)** and Margaret Hay **(15)**. In the summer of 1610, three years after her father's third marriage, fifteen-year-old Isobel was married to John Maitland, 2nd Lord Thirlestane.[3] Astute and hardworking, with a reputation for integrity, he had followed his father into a public career, becoming a Privy Councillor and a Lord of Session. He was created Viscount of Lauderdale in 1616 and was further elevated in 1624 when he became 1st Earl of Lauderdale.[4]

Isobel and he had their family home at Lethington Tower (now Lennoxlove), where he began an extensive building programme,[5] but his duties often took them to Edinburgh too, and in 1612-13 repairs were being made to Lady Thirlestane's seat in St Giles'. This was evidently a long term commitment, for in 1631-32 three wrights spent three days putting up the now Earl and Countess of Lauderdale's seat at a cost of £5:12/-, probably in the East Kirk, with a lock and key costing 20/-. If they were indeed sharing the same pew, that was unusual.[6]

Isobel's maternal relatives had been staunch members of the Reformed Church of Scotland and it seems likely that she herself was devout. Her husband went on to become a supporter of the Covenanters and their pious daughter Jane had apparently just finished copying out the entire Bible when she died at the age of nineteen in 1631. Despite the fact that the Reformers disapproved of funeral services, especially those with sermons praising the dead, John Maitland, presumably a relative, preached a lengthy sermon at Jane's funeral in St Mary's Church, Haddington on 19 December. This was published two years later, with an elegy by William Drummond of Hawthornden the well-known poet attached.[7] Little is known of Isobel's daily life, but she seems to have participated in the Maitland family's literary tradition, for she was celebrated in eulogistic terms both by Drummond and the Scottish poet Arthur Johnston.[8]

Isobel died at Lethington Tower on 2 November 1638 at the age of 44 years, 3 months and 2 days after a very long and trying illness. She too was buried in the Maitland family vault in St Mary's Church, Haddington. The Latin epitaph on her tomb describes how she had lived with her husband 'in wonderful concord for 28 years and 4 months', and 'blessed him with 15 children'. Of their seven sons and eight daughters, only two sons and one daughter survived, and the epitaph explains that her sorrowing husband erected the monument to himself and his 'incomparable wife, whose merits no love could match.'[9] It bears alabaster effigies of them both, similar to those on the adjoining memorial to his parents. (Plate 5) Isobel's eldest son John would find lasting fame, for he was none other than the famous 1st Duke of Lauderdale who became the immensely powerful Secretary of State for Scotland after the Restoration of King Charles II in 1660.

---

[1] *Scots Peerage*, iii, 372

[2] NRS, Wills and Testaments, Edinburgh Commissary Court CC8/8/44/635-637 (Lilias Drummond)

[3] Epitaph on her monument in St Mary's Church, Haddington; *RMS 1609-1620*, ed. John Maitland Thomson (Edinburgh 1892), 116, no. 307

[4] Brunton, *Lords of Session*, 260-262

[5]*Scots Peerage*, v, 301-302; Rosalind K. Marshall, 'A History of Lennoxlove' in Lennoxlove Conservation Plan (June 2002), 23-24

[6] ECA, MS Dean of Guild Accounts 1568-1626, 1631-1632 n/p

[7] J. Maitland, *A Funerall Sermonn, Preached at the Buriall of the Lady Jane Maitland, daughter of the Right Noble Earle, John, Earle of Lauderdale, at Haddington, the 19 of December 1631* (Edinburgh 1633); James Miller, *The Lamp of Lothian or The History of Haddington* (Edinburgh 1844), 426-427; Steven J. Reid, David McOmish, *Neo-Latin Literature and Literary Culture in Early Modern Scotland* (Brill 2016), 184-185; *Poems of William Drummond of Hawthornden* (Maitland Club 1832), 295

[8] George Seton, *Memoir of Alexander Seton, Earl of Dunfermline* (Edinburgh 1882), 150

[9] *The Historical Works of Sir James Balfour*, ii, 69; Miller, *Lamp of Lothian*, 426-427. The effigies of Isabel and her husband are on the right. See Plate 5. Translation of the Latin epitaph by Roy Pinkerton

# 13

## *Juliana Ker, Countess of Haddington*

Seen in a miniature of 1625, Juliana Ker appears much as she would have done when she sat in her seat in St Giles'. Red-haired and with rather a large nose, she wears a smart black hat with jewelled hat band, a falling ruff in the current style and, suspended from her right ear, a long, thin, plait of hair, presumably that of her husband, again in the latest fashion.[1] Now in her late forties, she would have been raised in Ferniehirst Castle, near Jedburgh, for she was the daughter of its owner, Sir Thomas Ker, and his wife Janet Kirkcaldy. However, Sir Thomas and his father-in-law Sir William Kirkcaldy of Grange were staunch supporters of Mary, Queen of Scots, and Juliana's childhood was complicated by their efforts on behalf of the imprisoned Queen. As a result, her father's lands were forfeited and he spent several years in exile. Her grandfather, Kirkcaldy, was hanged.[2]

Juliana must have been born in the 1570s and by 1588 she was the wife of Sir Patrick Hume of Polwarth.[3] Their country home was at Redbraes Castle, now a fragmentary ruin, near Duns in Berwickshire, but her husband was regularly in Edinburgh, for he was Master of the Royal Household, a Gentleman of the Bedchamber and a well-known Court poet.[4] He and Juliana had five sons, Patrick, Thomas, John, James and George, along with three daughters, Elizabeth, Jean and Sophia **(38)** and when he made his Will at Redbraes on 5 March 1602 it contained an unusually fervent tribute. 'I leave my loving and affectionate heart with the blessing of God to my dear and only best beloved bedfellow and dearest spouse', he wrote, making Juliana his sole executrix and guardian of their children. This, he said, was in respect of her good and gentle behaviour and the godly and honest duty she paid to him in all respects, 'to his comfort and exceeding joy'. He died on 15 June 1609.[5]

Fortunately some of Juliana's letters have survived to show us that there was more to her than meek wifely behaviour. As a widow, she had a liferent of Redbraes Castle, and although she usually lived in Edinburgh, she kept a close eye on her jointure lands there, complaining bitterly in 1613 that all her corn in The Merse had been spoiled by the bad weather as a result of 'the malice of that godless [local] minister', although she did not explain what he had done, or failed to do.[6] That same year she married in Edinburgh Sir Thomas Hamilton, Secretary of State, a widower twice over with ten children. It has been suggested that his choice owed much to the fact that Juliana's brother, Robert, Earl of Somerset, was high in the favour of James VI, and indeed, only six months after his third marriage, Hamilton was made Lord Binning, then Earl of Melrose and finally 1st Earl of Haddington. He became Lord President of the Court of Session and accumulated great wealth, but his rise to power cannot of course be attributed solely to the connection Juliana brought him, for he was an astute and extremely hard working statesman.[7] He was also known for his despotic manner and 'choleric constitution'[8], but Juliana was equal to that, telling him sharply on one occasion that nothing would move her to humble herself so much to any man living as she had done and would willingly do to him.[9]

Within a few weeks of their wedding, when he had to go to London, she plied him with indignant letters from Edinburgh in her vigorous italic writing.[10] He had written to her several times on his way south, but far from consoling her for his absence, his messages brought her 'great heaviness' she said, since he was ready to risk himself on long journeys by land and sea. 'Therefore, my sweet bird, as you love me, or desire to bring any joy to my heart, mend these faults.'[11] Another reproachful letter was probably written in 1615 when she pregnant with their only child together. She had been very sick and fearful since he went away, and when she was dead, she said, 'ye will weep for the abuse of such love.'[12] This late baby was born safely, although she was very ill afterwards, and they named him Robert, no doubt after her brother.[13]

They stayed in a large house in the Cowgate, just down the slope from St Giles', where the supporting southern pillars of George IV Bridge now stand. It was leased from Sir James McGill, along with a coach house and back yard. Their men and women servants were accommodated in two separate rented properties nearby.[14] Juliana would have been a regular attender at St Giles'. She was given her own seat there in 1614, the year of her second marriage and her letters provide evidence of firm religious belief.[15] She continued to make visits to her jointure lands in the Borders, and in 1634 she was telling George, her youngest son by her first marriage, that he was welcome to East Mains where she used only the low chamber, an addition built on by a previous owner when he was too old to occupy the main house. She kept no more than a bed and coffer there for her visits. George had apparently been complaining that she had removed some of the furniture from Redbraes Castle, which her liferent did not entitle her to do. She told him briskly not to storm about that, for she had taken away only her bed and the one used by her gentlewoman and her chambermaid who both slept beside her.[16]

Travelling to the Borders was a trial. Her coach was not always available and she complained that she did not have good horses.[17] She was even more dissatisfied with her chamberlain, who oversaw her lands there, exclaiming in 1635, 'The devil reward him!' when he had not seen to the proper thatching of the main house at Redbraes.[18] She fell into severe financial difficulties,[19] and even more infuriating was the behaviour of her eldest son, Patrick. In 1636 she heard that he was living in his house with a servant woman who was not the wife he had recently married. She prayed that God would forgive him, adding that he seemed not to be aware of the sin that he was committing, and brushed aside her advice as though she were a Turk or pagan. With a grieved heart she prayed for him every day, and ordered George to tell the minister to speak to Patrick and get him to dismiss that 'arrant whore'.[20]

The previous year she had rebuked George himself over his choice of name for his newborn son. Although she was glad that the boy had now been christened, he had ignored the message she sent him by Master Robert, to the effect that the baby should be given a Hume family name. However, when she heard that his wife was seriously unwell after the birth, she tried to consult the famous Dr David Arnot, who was a fellow member of St Giles', but he had not been in the kirk for eight days past because he was ill, and indeed died that November. However, drawing on her own experience after the birth of Robert, she urged George not to let his wife go to the church either on foot or horseback until the weather was milder, but to keep herself well from crab and cold, as his dear father [the long dead Sir Patrick Hume] used to say to her.[21]

Juliana had been ill herself and she died early in March 1637. She was buried at Holyrood on the 30th, without any of the funeral ceremonial which those of the Reformed faith condemned. Her husband died on 29 May that same year.[22]

---

[1] Miniature by an unknown artist, in a private collection; illustrated in black and white in Rosalind K. Marshall, *Childhood in Seventeenth-Century Scotland* (National Galleries of Scotland, Edinburgh 1976), 41

[2] *Scots Peerage*, v, 62-69; Maureen M. Meikle, 'Ker, Sir Thomas, of Ferniehirst', *ODNB* (Oxford University Press 2004)

[3] NRS, GD158/190, Papers of the family of Hume of Polwarth, Berwickshire, Earls of Marchmont, mentioning disposition of lands of Harden to Patrick Hume and Juliana Ker in 1588

[4] *Scots Peerage*, vi, 19-20; Michael R.G. Spiller, 'Hume, Sir Patrick, of Polwarth', *ODNB* (Oxford University Press 2004); William Fraser, *Memorials of the Earls of Haddington* (Edinburgh 1889), i, 286-7

[5] NRS, Wills and Testaments, Edinburgh Commissary Court, CC8/8/46/688-693 (Patrick Hume)

[6] Fraser, op. cit., ii, 123; probably Alexander Home, minister of Eccles, *Fasti Ecclesiae Scoticanae* ed. Hew Scott, (Edinburgh 1917), 12, to whom she had written about estate finances in 1615; NRS, GD158/2799, Papers of the family of Hume of Polwarth, Berwickshire, Earls of Marchmont

[7] *Scots Peerage*, iv, 310-315; Julian Goodare, 'Hamilton, Thomas, earl of Melrose and first earl of Haddington', *ODNB* (Oxford University Press), 2004; Fraser, op. cit., 36

[8] *Scot of Scotstarvet*, (Edinburgh 1872), 74; Fraser, op. cit. i, 181-182

[9] Fraser, op. cit., ii, 125

[10] Rosalind K. Marshall, *Virgins and Viragos: A History of Women in Scotland from 1080-1980* (London and Chicago 1983), 65, 89-90, 104, 145-146, 167

[11] Fraser, op. cit., ii, 123-4

[12] Ibid., ii, 124-125

[13] NRS, Papers of the family of Hume of Polwarth, Berwickshire, Earls of Marchmont, GD158/2697/13/4

[14] *Edinburgh Housemails Taxation Book,* 497, 529, 530, 534

[15] ECA, MS Dean of Guild Accounts 1568-1626, April 1614, n/p

[16] NRS, Hume of Polwarth, GD158/2697/13/13

[17] Fraser, op. cit., ii, 123

[18] NRS, Hume of Polwarth, GD158/2697/13/17

[19] Fraser, op. cit., i, 36

[20] NRS, Hume of Polwarth, GD158/2834; GD158/2697/13/36

[21] NRS, Hume of Polwarth, GD158/2697/14/4; *Edinburgh Burgh Extracts 1626-41,* 79

[22] *Scots Peerage,* iv, 313-314; Fraser, *op. cit.,* ii, 82-83

# 14

## *Elizabeth Bellenden, Lady Ormiston*

Elizabeth Bellenden came from an old established Edinburgh legal family. Her father, Sir John Bellenden of Auchnoull, lived in the Canongate, as his ancestors had done for generations. He was Lord Justice Clerk, a position which he had inherited in 1547 from his father, Thomas Bellenden, and which would eventually pass to his son, Lewis, when Sir John himself died in 1576. Elizabeth and her younger sister Annabella **(17)** were the children of his third wife, Janet Seton.[1] Probably born in the late 1560s, Elizabeth was at first married to a country laird, James Lawson of Humbie, in East Lothian. Little is known about him, not even the date of his death, but he owned a tower house later described as The Old Place, fifteen miles from Edinburgh. It no longer exists. He and Elizabeth had various children whose names are not all recorded but they included a son, Robert, and two daughters, Janet and Elizabeth.[2]

Elizabeth's half-brother Sir Lewis Bellenden died in 1591 in somewhat strange circumstances, according to Scot of Scotstarvet, that famous purveyor of gossiping anecdotes. Out of curiosity, he said, Sir Lewis persuaded Richard Graham, a well-known sorcerer, to come into his yard in the Canongate and raise the devil. This the sorcerer did to such effect that Sir Lewis later died of shock. Whatever the truth of that, the man appointed as his successor as Lord Justice Clerk was not another Bellenden but Elizabeth's second husband, Sir John Cockburn of Ormiston.[3]

A widower, Cockburn came from the same tight little Edinburgh legal circle as the Bellendens. Already an Extraordinary Lord of Session and knighted in 1591, he was noted the following year for his longstanding faithful service to James VI, often at his own great expense, and in 1593 he would become an Ordinary Lord of Session, as Lord Ormiston[4]. The first mention that Elizabeth and he had married comes in a legal document of 1605, when it was argued by the defence that he could not take part in the trial of a man charged with mutilation, because the victim was a tenant of 'My Lady Humbie, spouse to My Lord Justice Clerk'.[5] Whatever the date of their wedding, Elizabeth and he went on to have several daughters, the eldest named Katherine,[6] and Ormiston's eldest son John, by his first marriage, later married Elizabeth's daughter from her first marriage, Elizabeth Lawson.[7]

It was as Lady Ormiston that Elizabeth was granted her seat in St Giles' in the winter of 1608/9.[8] Her husband was considerably older than herself, and by the end of 1622, he was reported as being so afflicted with extreme age, blindness and other infirmities that he could not go out or discharge his duties as Lord Justice Clerk.[9] Four years later, on 2 September 1626, he made his Will and died on 12 October. His sole executor was to be his 'well deserving and beloved bedfellow Dame Elizabeth Bellenden'. She was to deal with all his goods, sums of money, silver work, furniture and furnishings, selling and disposing of them 'at her pleasure', for the good of their family and neighbours, and with the advice of several friends who included Adam, Bishop of Dunblane. One of the witnesses was Elizabeth's son Robert Lawson, by now a graduate and possibly a lawyer. Lord Ormiston's goods were valued at £6834 Scots, but his debts outweighed this total by almost £50. They consisted mainly of fees owed to a long list of servants, past and present, including his cook and 'the old nurse', as well as ministers' stipends and a number of annualrents.[10]

Elizabeth lived for another eight years, dying in her Edinburgh house in August 1630. Tantalisingly, although her son Robert registered the valuation of her estate on 6 October that year, the relevant pages are missing from the Edinburgh Register of Testaments. However, we know that her Testament had existed, because it is noted in the Register's Minute Book of the time. It did not include a personal Will written by herself,[11] but the second Testament covering omissions from the first has survived. This gives an interesting glimpse of her lifestyle, listing as it does those of her furnishings which had been left out of the previous Testament.

As well as her house in Edinburgh, Elizabeth in her widowhood had the liferent of her late husband's houses in Humbie and Ormiston, the result of her marriage contracts. She had obviously retained many of their furnishings, for each of these residences was plentifully supplied with walnut and wainscot beds, feather mattresses and pairs of linen sheets, blankets and pillows. There were six great trunks containing taffeta covers, and there were many pairs of taffeta curtains of varied colours, some embroidered and most with expensive silk fringes. The Edinburgh house had a large table, 12 linen tablecloths, 4 more of a coarser linen, and dozens of 'serviettes'. More important was the silverware missed from the inventories of the three houses: two silver gilt basins and two more with matching lavers [ewers], two silver mazers [large cups] and two silver gilt cups along with dozens of pewter trenchers [plates], which would have been used by the servants. In all, the additional items were valued at £4583:4/- Scots.[12] After her husband's death Elizabeth had obviously continued to live in their fashionable and comfortable surroundings.

[1] NRS, Wills and Testaments, CC8/8/6/382 (Sir John Bellenden); Gordon Donaldson, *Scotland: James V to James VII* (Edinburgh 1965), 218; *Scots Peerage*, ii, 63-70

[2] *The Register of the Great Seal of Scotland 1609-1620* ed. John Maitland Thomson (Edinburgh 1892), 64, 478; op. cit. *1620-1633*, 14

[3] Scot of Scotstarvet, 104; Brunton, *Lords of Session*, 216-7

[4] NRS, Records of the Parliaments of Scotland, PA2/14, 53, Ratification to Sir John Cockburn of the barony of Ormiston; *Letters and State Papers Illustrative of the Reign of James VI* (Abbotsford Club 1838), 261n; Brunton, *Lords of Session*, 216-217

[5] Robert Pitcairn, *Ancient Criminal Trials in Scotland*, ii, Part 2 (1600-1609), (Bannatyne Club 1833), 458-459; *Scots Peerage*, ii, 68

[6] *The Register of the Great Seal of Scotland A.D. 1620-1633*, ed. John Maitland Thomson (Edinburgh 1892), 121

[7] *Scots Peerage*, vi, 596

[8] ECA, MS Dean of Guild Accounts 1568-1626, 21 November 1608-19 February 1609, n/p

[9] Robert and Harry A. Cockburn, *The Records of the Cockburn Family* (London and Edinburgh 1913), 122-123

[10] NRS, Wills and Testaments, Edinburgh Commissary Court, CC8/8/54/37-43 (John Cockburn)

[11] *Commissariat Record of Edinburgh Testaments 1601-1700*, ed. Francis J. Grant, (Scottish Record Society 1898), 6 (Prefaratory Note) and 25, listed as 'Bannatyne, Dame Elizabeth, Lady Ormestoun, elder'

[12] NRS, Wills and Testaments, Edinburgh Commissary Court, CC8/8/56/200-207 (Elizabeth Bellenden)

# 15

## *Margaret Hay, Countess of Dunfermline*

In 1607, eighteen months after the death of Grizel Leslie **(4)**, Lord Chancellor Dunfermline married again. His new wife, Margaret Hay, was fifteen and he was fifty-one. Once more, he had chosen a Protestant bride. Margaret was the daughter of James, 7th Lord Hay of Yester and her devout mother Margaret Ker, Lady Yester **(24)**, would go on to found in Edinburgh a Presbyterian parish church which was named after her.[1]

We know what Margaret Hay looked like, for a handsome portrait of her survives, painted in London in 1615 by the leading Court artist, the Flemish Marcus Gheeraerts. Her outfit is not quite what she would have worn as she sat in her pew in St Giles', for she is dressed for a prestigious social occasion. Not only is she wearing a most elaborate embroidered and lace-trimmed dress with a farthingale skirt in the latest fashion, but her jewellery is magnificent: diamonds in her hair, round her neck and wrists and on her bodice.[2] (Plate 3)

Some of her letters survive too, one mentioning her small son Charles, triumphantly born the year after her marriage. In 1614 she wrote to a friend, apologising for not replying sooner to her letter. When she had received it, she said, she was so grieved at her son's sickness, fearing the worst, that she could not write to anyone. However, 'thanks to God', he was now well again.[3] The couple also had a daughter. Grizel, born in 1609, was obviously named after Grizel Leslie. A second daughter, Mary, born in 1611, did not survive,[4] but when she made her visit to London in 1615 Margaret was pregnant again. That November, summoned to Court by James VI, the Chancellor excused himself because 'my bedfellow is on the point to be brought to bed within very few days'. By the time that Margaret had recovered sufficiently for him to leave her, he said, he really could not make the long journey, for it would be the dead of winter 'and I am now no chicken'. There is not any record of that baby having survived and Margaret had no more children.[5]

When she and her husband were in Edinburgh, he sat in the East Kirk and she would probably have occupied her predecessor's seat there.[6] On 10 May 1616, however, Edinburgh Town Council granted them a second seat, this time in the Auld Kirk. It was to be on the east side of the Provost's Loft, 'together with the seat built for his [Dunfermline's] lady on the north side of his seat and contiguous to the seat built under the said Provost's loft for the Dean of Guild'. Ever since James VI's departure to London in 1603, there had been rumours that he would revisit his homeland, and at last this was imminent. In 1617, when the King once more occupied his carved and gilded Royal Pew in the Great Kirk, it was only fitting that the Chancellor and his lady should be close at hand.[7] They spent much of their time at his houses in Dalgety and at Pinkie, with its famous Renaissance painted ceilings, which he commissioned during his marriage to Margaret[8]. It was while he was staying there that he fell ill on 1 June 1622, dying between six and seven in the morning on the 16th of that same month.[9] A few days earlier he had added a codicil to his 1620 Will, making careful arrangements for his young family. Charles and his half-sister Jean were to be brought up by his favourite nephew, George, 3rd Earl of Winton, but

Margaret could keep her daughter, 11-year-old Grizel, if she so desired. She did not, however, and Grizel was brought up by Winton with her brother.[10]

Margaret's financial situation had been settled in her marriage contract. She would have the liferent of the houses at Pinkie and Dalgety, which meant that she would have the use of the properties but would not be able to dispose of them, because after her death they would pass to her husband's heir. At his own wish, the Chancellor's funeral took place at Dalgety, far removed from any of the worldly pomp 'which all that knows me may know I never liked.'[11] In fact, it was a magnificent occasion, the long procession led by a group of 25 poor men followed by his various attendants, trumpeters and heralds, a huge number of male dignitaries marching along after them. His coffin was carried to St Bridget's Church and placed beside those of his first two wives.[12]

Margaret was now a very wealthy widow but eleven years later, in 1633, at the age of 41, she unexpectedly married James Livingston, an officer in the Scottish Brigade in the Netherlands. He was immediately granted the title of Lord Livingston of Almond and in 1641 was created 1st Earl of Callendar.[13] By a special letter from the King, Margaret at her own request was allowed to keep her superior title and precedence as Countess of Dunfermline.[14] This was not unusual. How her relationship with Livingston developed is unrecorded, but his public progress was highly erratic, as he veered between his loyalty to Charles I and his support of the Covenanters, now fleeing the country, now returning, suffering periods of imprisonment and having his estates confiscated.[15]

Rather than living at his house of Callendar, Margaret seems to have spent much of her time at Dalgety, repeatedly suing her son Charles, 2nd Earl of Dunfermline over her financial rights.[16] Her loft above the family burial vault in St Bridget's Church bore the large coat of arms of her first husband and in 1649 she was rebuked by Dalgety Kirk Session for placing what were described as 'idolatrous and superstitious images' in the church's glass windows, stained glass having been banned since the Reformation. She was also forbidden to introduce any such 'novelties' without first informing the local presbytery of her intentions, and she was later charged with scandalous conduct in 'tarrying at home upon the Lord's Day' rather than going to the kirk.[17] Perhaps we can see in these events some echo of her first husband's religious views. When she died on 30 December 1659, at the age of 66, she was buried beside him and his two former ladies.[18] From her early days as a naïve young bride, she had become a forceful personality and, composing her epitaph, the poet James Watson praised her as the Phoenix of her Sex, asking

'...what had she been

Had She been He, a soul so masculine'.[19]

[1] *Scots Peerage*, viii, 444-449

[2] Portrait of Margaret Hay, Countess of Dunfermline by Marcus Gheeraerts the younger, 1615 (Dunedin Public Art Gallery, Collections). See Plate 3

[3] Bruce Gordon Seton, *The House of Seton: A Study of Lost Causes* (Edinburgh 1939), 305; W. Fraser, *Memorials of the Montgomeries, Earls of Eglinton* (Edinburgh 1859), 194

[4] Seton, *op. cit.*, 305; George Seton, *Memoir of Alexander Seton, Earl of Dunfermline* (Edinburgh 1892), 153-162

[5] Seton, *Memoir*, 114

[6] ECA, MS Dean of Guild Accounts 1568-1626, n/p 1608, n/p 1612-13

[7] *Edinburgh Burgh Extracts 1606-1626*, 142; Seton, *Memoir*, 114, 123-124

[8] Michael Bath, *Renaissance Decorative Painting in Scotland* (National Museums of Scotland 2003), 79-102, 231-236

[9] *The History of the House of Seytoun by Sir Richard Maitland of Lethington, Knight* ed. John Fullarton (Maitland Club 1829), 101

[10] *Scots Peerage*, iii, 373

[11] Seton, *Memoir*, 156-160; NRS, Wills and Testaments, Edinburgh Commissary Court, CC8/8/53/241-256 (Alexander Seton, 1st Earl of Dunfermline)

[12] 'The Funeral of Alexander, Earl of Dunfermline' in *The Scottish Antiquary, or Northern Notes and Queries*, xiii, no. 52 (April 1899), 160-168

[13] *Scots Peerage*, ii, 360-363

[14] *The Register of the Privy Council of Scotland*, 2nd series, vii, 1638-43, ed. David Masson and Peter Hume Brown, (Edinburgh 1906), 16

[15] David Stevenson, 'Livingston, James, first earl of Callendar', *ODNB* (Oxford University Press 2004); William Maxwell Morison, *The Decisions of the Court of Session from its First Institution to the Present Time*, v, (Edinburgh 1802), 4078-4081; NRS, SIG1/38/11, signature of the lands of Callendar etc granted to Margaret, Countess of Dunfermline (1639, when her husband went to France)

[16] Bruce Gordon Seton, op. cit., 306

[17] Seton, *Memoir*, 146, 161

[18] *The Diary of Mr John Lamont of Newton 1649-1671*, ed. George R. Kinloch (Maitland Club 1830), 119; George Seton, op. cit., 147

[19] *James Watson's Choice Collection of Comic and Serious Scots Poems*, ed. H. H. Wood (Scottish Text Society 1977), 39-40

# 16

## Margaret Haliburton, Viscountess Dupplin

The daughter of Sir James Haliburton and his wife Margaret Scrimgeour, Margaret Haliburton and her siblings, who included her sister Magdalene **(18)**, would have been brought up in their father's handsome medieval tower house at Pitcur, near Blairgowrie in Perthshire.[1] Her first husband, Patrick Ogilvy, was heir to the nearby estate of Inchmartin, and she and he had four children, Andrew, Marjorie and Elizabeth, along with the fourth, whose name does not appear in the records.[2] Patrick, however, did not live to enjoy his inheritance, for he died on 21 November 1592 while his father was still alive.

Margaret handed over his Testament for registration four years later after an unexplained delay. It reveals that they had been living quietly in the country without any obvious involvement in public life. Her husband's moveable possessions were estimated at only £369 and included his grey horse worth £24, another horse worth almost half as much, which was probably used by his wife, and an old horse worth only a few merks. Otherwise, his assets consisted of various crops of oats and pease in his barn, and there were a number of rents and fees owed to him by his tenants. The family servants included Bessie Bruce and Elizabeth Robson, who would have to be paid 10 merks and 4 merks respectively for their employment during the year of his death.[3]

We do not know the date of Margaret's second marriage, but by 15 November 1595 she had become the wife of

George Hay, her first husband's cousin.[4] Hay had been brought up as a Roman Catholic and educated at the Scots College in Pont-à-Mousson in Lorraine where his uncle was rector. Home again, he outwardly conformed to Protestantism.[5] He then obtained a monopoly of glass manufacture in Scotland, followed by a monopoly of whaling. His business affairs were extremely lucrative and he was able to accumulate various substantial properties including the handsome Gowrie House in Perth, where he added a painted ceiling with his coat of arms to their little banqueting house on the banks of the River Tay.[6] Meanwhile, Margaret went on to have three children with him: Peter, George and Margaret[7].

Her husband then became involved in politics for the first time, with his appointment in 1616 as Lord Clerk Register and a member of the Scottish Privy Council.[8] It was in the following January that Margaret obtained her own seat in St Giles' as 'the Lady Clerk Register'.[9] James VI was to pay his promised return visit to Scotland that year, and she and her husband would have to be present when the King attended church services in Edinburgh. During the royal visit, it was noticed that Hay took Communion at Holyrood 'after the English form' favoured by the King, kneeling rather than seated in the Presbyterian manner and as late as 1620 he was suspected of being involved in correspondence with a Catholic source. However, his successful career remained unaffected and in 1622 he rose to the pre-eminent position of Lord Chancellor.[10]

That same year, Margaret was granted the lands of Over Kinfauns, near Perth[11] but by then the couple must have been spending significant amounts of time in Edinburgh. In 1623, as 'the Chancellor's wife', Margaret and he were both given new wainscot seats in St Giles'. Her seat and that of

*1 St Giles' Cathedral interior, 2019, looking towards the East End
(Photograph © Peter Backhouse)*

**2** *Marcus Gheeraerts the Younger,* Alexander Seton, 1st Earl of Dunfermline *(National Galleries of Scotland, PG2176. Purchased 1970)*

**3** *Marcus Gheeraerts the Younger,* Margaret Hay, Countess of Dunfermline, *1615, oil on canvas (Collection of the Dunedin Public Art Gallery) (also on front cover)*

**4** *Above: The Lauderdale Monument, St Mary's Parish Church, Haddington (The Trustees of the Lauderdale Aisle; photograph © Peter Backhouse)*

**5** *Below: detail of the Lauderdale Monument, effigy of Lady Thirlestane and her husband on the left (The Trustees of the Lauderdale Aisle; photograph © Peter Backhouse)*

**6** *Above: The Lady Yester memorial, Greyfriars Kirk, Edinburgh (photograph © Peter Backhouse)*

**7** *Below: King David playing his harp, ceiling panel from Dean House, Edinburgh, home of Katherine Dick, Lady Nisbet (© National Museums of Scotland)*

8 *Adam de Colone ?1572–1651; portrait of* Lady Margaret Livingstone,
2nd Countess of Wigtown, *1625; Tate, presented by Tate Patrons 2011;
photograph © Tate*

**9** *George Jamesone*, Lady Mary Erskine, Countess Marischal, *1626*
*(National Galleries of Scotland, NG 958. Purchased 1908)*

**10** *Dunottar Castle, home of Lady Mary Erskine, Countess Marischal (photograph © Peter Backhouse)*

the Provost's wife were 'reformed' (meaning altered) shortly afterwards.[12] Margaret also gained an impressive new title when Hay was created Viscount Dupplin in 1626 and she became a Viscountess. Three years later he was said to be old and infirm, but as active as ever. Margaret, however, died on 4 April 1633, and was buried in Kinnoull Church, a few weeks before her husband became Earl of Kinnoull on 25 May.[13] He would die in London on 19 August 1635, but his body was brought back to Kinnoull, where his imposing life-size memorial effigy dominates the church interior.[14]

---

[1] *Scots Peerage*, iii, 313; v, 223; *The Royal Commission on the Ancient and Historical Monuments of Scotland. South-east Perth: an archaeological landscape* (Edinburgh 1994), 139, 141, 164

[2] NRS, Wills and Testaments, CC8/8/28/715-716 (Patrick Ogilvy)

[3] Ibid., 715

[4] *Scots Peerage*, v, 221

[5] Julian Goodare, 'Hay, George, first earl of Kinnoull', *ODNB* (Oxford University Press 2004)

[6] Deborah Howard, 'The Kinnoull Aisle and Monument' in *Architectural History*, xxxix, (January 1996), 37

[7] *Scots Peerage*, v, 223

[8] Goodare, *ODNB* (Oxford University Press 2004)

[9] ECA, MS Dean of Guild Accounts 1568-1626, 1616-17, p.14

[10] Goodare, *ODNB* (Oxford University Press 2004)

[11] NRS, SIG1/75/3, Register of Signatures, 7 November 1622

[12] ECA, MS Dean of Guild Accounts, 1568-1626, year 1623-1624, p.11

[13] *Scots Peerage*, v, 220-223; Brunton, *Lords of Session*, 256-258

[14] Goodare, *ODNB* (Oxford University Press 2004)

# 17

## *Annabella Bellenden, Lady Lauder*

Annabella Bellenden was the younger sister of Elizabeth Bellenden, Lady Ormiston **(14)**. They were still very young when their father Sir John Bellenden, the Lord Justice Clerk, died and in his Will in 1576 he left the residue of his estate to be divided between them.[1] It was originally intended that Annabella should marry James, the Roman Catholic son of Sir William Maitland of Lethington, but James had other ideas and in 1587 he paid 8000 merks to escape from the arrangement so that he could marry the Catholic daughter of Lord Herries instead.[2]

A rejection of this kind was never good for the reputation of the spurned fiancée, and another ten years passed before a husband was found for Annabella. This may in part have been because the Maitland family appear to have had some continuing responsibility for providing a suitable bridegroom. James Maitland had several aunts not much older than himself. In 1586 one of them, Marie Maitland, had married the Protestant Alexander Lauder of Hatton, but she died in June 1596, leaving three young children, Richard, Jane and Helen. Shortly afterwards, her widower married Annabella.[3]

The Hatton estate was nine miles from Edinburgh, and Annabella's marriage contract gave her a liferent of Bruntsfield, now part of the city. The main house at Bruntsfield was at that time also occupied by her widowed mother-in-law, and when old Lady Lauder died, Lauder sold the property in 1603 and instead settled on his wife various other lands including Westhall and Ratho.[4] As well as bringing up her stepchildren, Annabella and her husband had two sons. Lewis, born in 1598, was named after her late half-brother, Sir Lewis Bellenden. George, two years younger than Lewis, became a lieutenant colonel in the service of the Dutch. His career would be spent abroad, and when he left his native land for the first time he wrote a poem fondly bidding Scotland farewell, wishing his mother joy and expressing the hope that she would 'long enjoy thy mate'.[5] There is no record of when Annabella joined her sister in having her own seat in St Giles', but in November 1613 a key was provided for it, the usual precaution for keeping out interlopers or vandals.[6]

Annabella's husband made his Will on 10 November 1627. He was sick in body, he said, and it became all Christians to put their houses in order to be ready for the Lord's Call. He described at some length his conventional Reformed belief that he would be one of the Elect, saved by the merits of the precious blood of Jesus Christ. The moveable goods he left and the debts owed to him amounted to just over £2000 Scots, but he owed over £8600, mostly for undisclosed reasons, but also for servants' wages and local taxes. He named two executors, 'my only beloved spouse Annabella Bellenden' and their son Lewis. Among the witnesses to his Testament was Annabella's nephew Robert Lawson. Lauder died just four days later.[7] Annabella's date of death is unknown but she was still alive in January 1629 when she made over to her elder son her liferent rights in the properties that he had inherited from his father.[8]

---

[1] NRS, Wills and Testaments, Edinburgh Commissary Court, CC8/8/6/382 (Sir John Bellenden)
[2] *Scots Peerage*, v, 295-6

[3] J. Stewart Smith, *The Grange of St Giles'* (Edinburgh 1898), 240-241

[4] Ibid., v, 241; *The Register of the Great Seal of Scotland 1609-1620*, ed. John Maitland Thomson (Edinburgh 1892), no. 137, p.50

[5] *Scots Peerage*, v, 243; NRS, Clerk Family of Penicuik Papers, GD18/294; *The Register of the Great Seal*, no. 326, p.122-123; Smith, *Grange of St Giles'*, 243

[6] ECA, MS Dean of Guild Accounts 1568-1626; November 1613, n/p

[7] NRS, Wills and Testaments, Edinburgh Commissary Court, CC8/8/54/409-414 (Alexander Lauder of Hatton)

[8] NRS, Clerk Family of Penicuik Papers GD18/299

# 18

## *Magdalene Haliburton, Countess of Ethie*

Magdalene Haliburton, daughter of Sir James Haliburton of Pitcur and Margaret Scrimgeour[1] was the younger sister of Margaret, Viscountess Dupplin **(16)**. On 4 December 1603 her marriage contract with John Erskine, the 11th Laird of Dun was signed[2] and they presumably lived on his Angus estate between Montrose and Brechin. They seem to have had no surviving children and the Laird died at 8 o'clock in the morning on 23 March 1610.[3] Magdalene had a liferent of the Mains of Dun[4], but she went back to live permanently in her father's house of Pitcur, near Blairgowrie, where a traumatic event occurred on 12 April 1611.

The previous evening, John Crichton of Airliewicht, his uncle and two other relatives, all of them armed, met at his Perthshire house 'in a most unlawful and unseemly manner'. They had heard that Magdalene's father was away from home, visiting the Mearns, and the following morning, Crichton and two of his companions rode to Pitcur, while the others went to Newtyle to await his summons. Magdalene's sister Jean and her husband the Laird of Fintry were visiting Pitcur at the time, and when Crichton arrived there he announced that he had business with Magdalene's father. He was welcomed in a friendly manner and entertained to dinner, which was served at about noon in those days. Afterwards, he invited Magdalene to go outside and watch him ride at the glove, a popular pastime. This meant that he would demonstrate his dexterity by mounting his horse and galloping rapidly with a spear in his hand which he would use to pick up a glove that he had thrown on to the ground. Jean decided to go too and, unsuspecting, they accompanied him outside.

At that, his armed accomplices suddenly appeared and together they violently put hands on Magdalene and bound her hand and foot. She struggled frantically to free herself, but four times they managed to throw her on to the back of one of their horses. When she continued to resist, they pointed their pistols at her breast, threatening with many horrible oaths to kill her as well as Jean and their servants who had come running up to help. Unable to carry out their plan, Crichton and his associates struck the two women many times 'to the effusion of our blood in great quantity', they reported. They tore off Magdalene's headdress, pulling plaits of hair from her head, before riding off, leaving their victims for dead. Magdalene was in no doubt that Crichton had intended to rape her, probably with the intention of forcing her into an unwanted marriage with him. The graphic details of the attack are recorded in the Register of the Privy Council, for on 24 April the King's Advocate, acting on behalf of Magdalene, Jean, their father and Fintry presented a supplication describing what had happened. The two women were still 'lying bedfast in great dolour and pain, not likely to convalesce' and they demanded that Crichton and the others be prosecuted for their heinous crime. The Privy Council immediately granted their request.[5]

Happily Magdalene did recover, and not long afterwards she married again.[6] Her new husband was Sir John Carnegie, who owned the barony of Ethie, near Arbroath. He was in his early thirties and, as a steadfast supporter of James VI, he had recently been knighted.

Magdalene moved to the House of Ethie, a substantial medieval keep with recent additions, taking along her oak bed which was carved with the initials of her first husband and herself. Safe and settled, she now went on to have three sons and five daughters, two of the girls being called Margaret and Jean, after her sisters, and the youngest named after herself.[7] Carnegie became Sheriff Principal of Forfar but also engaged in a very active parliamentary career in Edinburgh and was frequently at Court in London.[8] The date when Magdalene first received her seat in St Giles' is not recorded, but in 1619 it was being enlarged, possibly to accommodate some of her relatives or servants, and in the early 1620s it was mended, suggesting her continuing presence.[9]

Her second marriage was obviously a personal success, for when her husband made a Will on 17 February 1631 (somewhat prematurely, as it turned out, for he would not die until 1667) he nominated their eldest son as his only executor, adding a list of eleven friends and relatives who should advise him. The first was his 'well beloved spouse', who must always be one of any three entrusted with the task. She was also to enjoy untroubled the entire furnishings of his principal house, along with the furnishings of Overhouse of Ethie, its various crops and servants. He did this, he said, because of his confidence in her good and virtuous disposition, knowing that she would arrange to pass them on to their eldest boy after her death.[10]

A firm supporter of Charles I against the Covenanters, Carnegie was arrested trying to flee to France shortly after the 1638 Glasgow General Assembly, but he was soon released and in 1639 was raised to the peerage with the title of Lord Lour. Finally, in 1647, Magdalene became a Countess when her husband was created Earl of Ethie, a title which he would subsequently exchange for that of Earl of Northesk.[11] They would have been in their sixties by then and, three years later, Magdalene predeceased him, dying at Ethie on 10 March 1650.[12]

---

[1] *Scots Peerage*, iii, 313; v, 223, vi, 495

[2] NRS, Papers of the Erskine Family of Dun, GD123/141

[3] *The Miscellany of the Spalding Club*, iv, (Aberdeen 1849), p. lxxviii; Robert Woodrow, *Collections upon the Lives of the Reformers and Most Eminent Ministers of the Church of Scotland*, i, (Maitland Club 1834), 440

[4] Assignation by Agnes Ogilvy, Lady Logy to Dame Margaret Haliburton, Lady Carnegie, 8 January 1614 in *Miscellany, Spalding Club*, vi (Aberdeen 1849), 81-2

[5] *The Register of the Privy Council of Scotland*, ed. P. Hume Brown, series ii, vol. viii (1544-1660), (Edinburgh 1908), 318

[6] The actual date is unknown

[7] *Scots Peerage*, vi, 495-497; Dundee City Archive and Record Centre, GD130/Box 7/XIII

[8] William Fraser, *History of the Carnegies, Earls of Southesk and of their Kindred*, (Edinburgh 1867), ii, 346

[9] Edinburgh City Archives, Dean of Guild MS Accounts 1568-1626, 11, 13

[10] Fraser, *History of the Carnegies*, ii, 352-3

[11] Ibid., 345-348; *Scots Peerage*, vi, 493-495

[12] Woodrow, op. cit., 440

# 19

## Margaret Houston, Lady Livingston

Margaret Houston came from Renfrewshire. Her father, John Houston, had inherited the lands of Houston there and sat in Parliament as a minor baron. Her mother was Margaret Stirling, daughter of Sir James Stirling of Keir. Houston Castle, the family home, was six miles north of Paisley and when Margaret's father died in 1609 he was buried with his ancestors beneath the chancel of the nearby medieval St Peter's Church.[1] Margaret's age at that time is not known, but she was probably a young teenager. She was certainly still single and it was not until July 1615 that she became the second wife of Sir William Livingston of Kilsyth, a middle-aged widower with a married daughter. His only son had died recently and his desire for a male heir was probably his motive for marrying a much younger woman.

Characterised by a contemporary as 'a man of parts and learning', Sir William had been knighted in 1594 and had become a member of the Privy Council in 1601. In 1609 he replaced Lord Balmerino as a Lord of Session and four years after that he was made Vice-Chamberlain of Scotland. Margaret and he had a son, James, who was born on 25 June 1616.[2] No doubt they would have divided their time between Sir William's medieval tower house, Kilsyth Castle in North Lanarkshire, and lodgings or property in Edinburgh.

On 10 February 1617 Margaret's seat was being made in St Giles', and in 1621-22 the sum of eighteen shillings was paid by the Dean of Guild for mending it.[3] Although her husband was known as a staunch royalist[4], she very likely had Covenanting sympathies, for on 12 August 1627, she was going to Cumbernauld Castle near Kilsyth to listen to Robert Bruce, the well-known former minister of St Giles'. He had lost his position and frequently been exiled for his outspoken criticism of James VI's insistence on having bishops within the Presbyterian Church of Scotland. On this occasion Bruce was going to preach to a group of ladies organised by his cousin, Margaret Livingston, Countess of Wigtown **(39),** no doubt making clear his opposition to Charles I's similar ecclesiastical policies. It is tempting to read some surprise into the Countess's remark that she and her mother as well as Lady Boyd and Lady Kilsyth would listen to Bruce, 'along with Kilsyth himself'.[5] Such informal gatherings were usually attended only by women, and Sir William's support for the monarchy was well-known. However, he was related to Bruce too, although more distantly, which may explain his presence. He may well have been in poor health by then, for he died a few weeks later.[6]

Free now to take a husband of her choice, in 1630 Margaret married John Cornwall, younger of Bonhard, who was about her own age.[7] The Cornwalls had originated in that English county during the Middle Ages, and were now a long-established family in West Lothian. John's great-grandfather, Nicholas Cornwall, had been a well-known Provost of Linlithgow, while his father, Walter, had represented his county in the Scottish Parliament of 1625. When Walter died sometime between 1635 and 1643, John inherited the family house and garden on the site of what now forms numbers 57-61 of Linlithgow High Street. The

Cornwall coat of arms with its motto 'We build you so verily' and the date 1571 is all that survives of it.[8]

Margaret's husband also owned Bonhard with its small sixteenth-century tower house three storeys high just outside Bo'ness. Nothing of it now remains, for it was burned down in 1959, its few remaining walls demolished in 1962. In Margaret's time, however, the large principal apartments on the first floor were decorated with the elegant plasterwork so fashionable in Scotland in the early seventeenth century. Immediately south of Bonhard were several pieces of land in Bonnington, which John also owned.[9]

Perhaps with some of the money Margaret brought with her from her first marriage, she and her husband were able to complete their ownership of Bonnington by purchasing an additional piece of land there in 1633. Ten years later, Bonnington was erected into a free barony by royal charter, bestowing it on both of them and their male heirs.[10] In fact, the couple had no sons, but they did have a daughter, called after her mother.[11] In that same year, 1643, John Cornwall was a Colonel of Horse in the Scottish Covenanting army, and from 1646-1649 he was a member of the Committee of War. He lived until 1666 or 1667. Margaret was still alive in 1643, when Bonnington became a free barony, but the date of her death is unknown.[12]

---

[1] William M. Metcalfe, *A History of the County of Renfrew from the Earliest Times* (Paisley 1905), 126

[2] *Scots Peerage* v, 190. The mention of a daughter, Margaret is probably a confusion with Margaret Houston's daughter with her second husband, *Scots Peerage*, vi, 591; Brunton, *Lords of Session*, 249; Livingston, James, of Barncloich, 1st Viscount Kilsyth, rev. Alison G. Muir, *ODNB* (Oxford University Press 2004); NRS, Papers of the

Graham Family, Dukes of Montrose, GD220/1/D/6/1/5, cancelled heritage bond

[3] ECA, MS Dean of Guild Accounts 1568-1626, 1617 p.16, (1626-1720), p.13

[4] Keith Brown, *Noble Power in Scotland from the Reformation to the Revolution* (Edinburgh 2013), 228

[5] Fraser, *Memorials of the Montgomeries*, i, 218

[6] Brunton, *Lords of Session*, 249

[7] *Scots Peerage*, ix, 90

[8] R.R. Stodart, *Genealogy of the Family of Cornwall of Bonhard* (London, 1877), 6; https://canmore.org.uk/site/214356/linlithgow-57-high-street

[9] Stodart, op. cit. 6; https://canmore.org.uk/site/49176/bonhard-house; Bonhard Castle,

https//www.scran.ac.uk/database/record.php?usi=000-000-511-132-C&

[10] *Register of the Great Seal of Scotland 1634-1657* ed. John Maitland Thomson (Edinburgh *1897*), no. 320, p.126; no. 1643, p.553

[11] *Scots Peerage*, vi, 591

[12] Stodart, op. cit., 6

# 20

## *Jean Hay, Countess of Mar*

Jean Hay was the daughter of that well-known Roman Catholic convert, Francis, 9th Earl of Erroll. Her mother, the Protestant Lady Elizabeth Douglas, was one of seven beautiful sisters known as 'the Pearls of Lochleven.' Their marriage had aroused a great deal of criticism because of his Catholicism, with Elizabeth's father being severely reprimanded for giving her to such an unsuitable husband. Erroll had, however, been determined to marry again, for both his previous wives had died young, leaving no children. Regardless of their difference in religion, he and Elizabeth settled down and proceeded to have no fewer than five sons and eight daughters. Jean was the second daughter.[1]

Her father's devotion to the Roman Catholic Church must have had a disturbing effect on Jean's childhood. Around the time when she was born, his imposing castle at Slains in Aberdeenshire was blown up on the orders of James VI because Erroll had been engaging in treasonable correspondence with Spain and was refusing to renounce his faith. He promptly had a magnificent new castle built near Cruden Bay. It came to be known as New Slains Castle, and he continued his activities undeterred. In 1608 the Church of Scotland excommunicated him and he was imprisoned, for neither the first time nor the last. In 1610, for instance, he was held in Edinburgh Castle, which may explain why, when Jean was married that same year to John

Erskine, heir to the 18th Earl of Mar, the ceremony took place there.

Erskine was a Protestant. He became a member of the Scottish Privy Council that year and in 1620 he was made an Extraordinary Lord of Session. That would probably have been when Jean was granted her own seat in St Giles', for the Dean of Guild accounts note that by 1621-22 repairs were being made to it at a cost of 24 shillings.[2] She and Erskine had four children, John, Francis, Elizabeth and Mary. It is interesting to note that her second son was called after her father who, when he made his Will in 1628, was still emphasising that he died as he had lived, 'a true and sincere apostolic Roman Catholic', and hoped that his children, his friends and everyone else would embrace Catholicism.[3]

Meanwhile, Jean's husband was struggling with his perennial financial difficulties. He had been granted a monopoly of tanning in Scotland, but this brought him more expense rather than a regular income and, perhaps for her future financial security, her father-in-law the 18th Earl of Mar granted Jean the lands of East Grange of Cambuskenneth in 1633. However, he died the following year and so Erskine at last inherited his titles, estates and houses, including Alloa Castle, Clackmannanshire, a massive fifteenth century tower house which was the principal family residence.[4] Jean was now Countess of Mar, and in subsequent years, her anxieties must have centred on political affairs rather than on their previous financial troubles. Her husband had been a Covenanter in 1638 but had since changed his allegiance to become an active royalist.[5] Her daughter Elizabeth, at an early age was married to the seventeen-year-old Master of Napier, a nephew of the royalist Marquis of Montrose. No problem with that would have been envisaged, but in 1644 Jean's son-in-law, his father and his brother-in-law were all placed by the Covenanters under what amounted to house arrest in their apartments in the Palace of Holyroodhouse. Worse was to follow, for when Elizabeth's husband managed to escape early the following year, she was imprisoned instead by Parliament in Edinburgh Castle, along with her seventeen-year-old sister-in-law, Lilias Graham.

Not only was that an alarming development, but in July 1645 Elizabeth and Lilias were begging for their release, complaining that 'they have long remained in close prison, none having access to them', and a widespread outbreak of the plague in Edinburgh had now spread to the Castle, adding 'great fear to their former uncomfortable state'. Their powerful friends came to the rescue, however, and on 24 July Parliament agreed that they could be held captive instead in the household of Elizabeth's parents. This must have come as a great relief to Jean and in the very next month, when the royalists were in the ascendant, the two young women were freed.[6]

During his final years, Jean's husband is said to have been blind. He made his Will on 20 May 1652, nominating her as his executor and leaving her all the jewels, silver and gold work, household plenishing and furniture in his houses, except of course for the heirship goods, which would pass automatically to their eldest son. He did this, he said, 'in testimony of her great care for him in his infirmity'. He died in 1653 or 1654.[7] Jean survived him, living at Alloa Castle and remaining particularly close to their younger daughter, Lady Mary, who was unmarried.

When she made her Will on 6 May 1664, Jean began with the conventional Protestant remarks about the uncertainty of the time of death making it advisable to arrange her affairs in advance so that she might concentrate on her change when it pleased the Lord to call her to heaven. She then named her 'well beloved daughter' Mary as her only executor, bequeathing to her all the goods, gear and money that she owned.[8] She died at Alloa on 24 May 1668, and £1666:13:4 Scots was paid for her funeral, including the cost of the mourning clothes and furnishings. Not only did a family wear black for months after an aristocratic death, but the main apartments of the deceased's houses were hung with black, sometimes for the rest of the widow's or widower's life. In all, the debts owed to Jean, meticulously listed by Mary, amounted to the large sum of £8537, mainly in the form of rents in kind, that is to say in barley, meal and so forth, from the tenants of the lands she owned. The debts that Jean herself owed were on several bonds and to various merchants, amounting to £8684. She had signed her Will 'with her own hand', and the clerk who copied it when her Testament was registered at Stirling Commissary Court on 25 September 1668 imitated her large, bold signature with its italic writing, the letter 'y' of her surname, Hay, ornamented with swirling loops.[9]

---

[1] *Scots Peerage*, vi, 374; iii, 574-577; Saenz, Concepcion. 'Hay, Francis, ninth earl of Erroll' in *ODNB* (Oxford University Press 2004)

[2] ECA, MS Dean of Guild Accounts 1568-1626, 1621-22, n/p

[3] *Scots Peerage*, iii, 576

[4] NRS, Papers of the Erskine Family, Earls of Mar and Kellie, GD124/1/120; https://canmore.org.uk/site/47167/alloa-tower

[5] Wells, V., 'Erskine, John, 19th or 3rd Earl of Mar' *ODNB* (Oxford University Press, 2004)

[6] Mark Napier, *Montrose and the Covenanters* (London 1838), 245; Mark Napier, *The Life and Times of Montrose* (Edinburgh 1840), 324; Ronald Williams, *The Heather and the Gale: Clan Donald and Clan Campbell*

*During the Wars of Montrose* (Colonsay, 1997), 159; NRS, The Records of the Parliaments of Scotland to 1707, PA2/23, f.278v

[7] *Scots Peerage*, v, 624; NRS, Papers of the Erskine Family, Earls of Mar and Kellie, GD124/3/51, 52

[8] Ibid., GD124/3/56; GD124/3/57

[9] NRS, Wills and Testaments, Stirling Commissary Court, CC21/5/7/721-724 (Jean Hay)

# 21

## *Marie Primrose, Lady Clerk*

Marie Primrose was the daughter of the eminent doctor, Gilbert Primrose, burgess of Edinburgh and official surgeon to James VI. Appointed in 1576, when the King was still a child, he would hold that office for the rest of his life.[1] He and his wife, Alison Graham, had several sons, including his namesake Gilbert, who became a leading Reformed minister in France[2], but Marie seems to have been their only and much younger daughter. In August 1588 she married David Gourlay, another Edinburgh burgess. She remained close to her father and she and Gourlay called their first child Gilbert, after him, then went on to have two more sons, Robert and David. Her husband died at some unknown date when their boys were still very small.[3]

Not surprisingly, Marie's parents took a close and protective interest in their fatherless grandsons, with her mother having a particular fondness for young Gilbert. This continued after Marie married for a second time, in March 1597. Her new husband was Alexander Clerk of Stenton, another merchant burgess of Edinburgh who was a widower with at least one son.[4] She and Clerk would have a son and a daughter, who were called after her parents, with the result that she now had one son named Gilbert Gourlay from her first marriage and another named Gilbert Clerk from her second. As well as staying in Edinburgh, the family lived for part of the time in Clerk's house in Stenton, East Lothian.

Forceful and energetic, in 1603 Marie's father accompanied James VI to London, where he was permanently based after that, becoming Chief Surgeon to the Royal Household there.[5] Before he left Scotland he made provision for Marie and her husband by giving to them securities and bonds for 20,000 merks Scots along with the revenues from his lands of Whitehouse.[6] His home would now be in King Street, Westminster, with an apartment at Whitehall where he continued his practice, employing his nephews, Duncan and Henry as his assistants.[7] Marie's mother may have preferred to remain in Edinburgh, close to her daughter and the grandchildren. She was certainly there in 1615 when she made her Will, leaving everything to her husband. She could not write, and so the notary signed her name, with her hand on the pen. This could have been because of illness, but it was a common enough situation for women who had simply never learned to write. One of her witnesses was Marie's first son, Gilbert Gourlay. Alison died in Edinburgh on 14 February 1616.[8]

Just two months later, on 18 April, Gilbert Primrose died in Westminster. His body was brought back to Edinburgh and he was buried in Greyfriars Churchyard, presumably beside his wife. The Latin epitaph on his gravestone recorded that he 'lived happily 80 years' and died 'adorned with Testimonies of Public Sorrow from Prince and People'.[9] His Will, which he had made five days earlier, throws light on his continuing relationship with Marie and the children of her first marriage. After recommending his soul to God, in the confidence that he would be safe and enjoy that perfect felicity in the kingdom of heaven appointed for all his chosen and Elect, he went on to explain that his wife, 'my loving bedfellow', had left everything to him. Knowing the great love that she had for their grandson Gilbert Gourlay and because of the love he himself had for Gilbert, he made him his only executor. In carrying out this role, young Gilbert was to pass on to Marie 'the best apparel' left by her mother, along with Alison's two belts of gold, two pairs of gold bracelets and a ring with a sapphire. She was to keep this jewellery for the use of her daughter, Alison Clerk.

Primrose felt that he had to explain that he was making no financial bequests to Marie and her husband because of his financial gifts to them when he had gone south. Now, they were to receive his silver gilt basin and ewer, a silver cup, a silver mazer, a silver salt and a dozen silver spoons, on condition that they must agree to renounce all other claims against him. He added, surely with some exaggeration, that this was all that he could do without taking from the Gourlay children the little he had provided for them, thereby exposing them to the hazard of begging for their bread. Moreover, Marie and Clerk must not contest his Will in any way but 'live in fatherly love' with the Gourlay children. If they did that, he would leave the couple his blessing. Did that suggest that there was jealousy between Marie's first sons and their stepfather? Perhaps.[10]

Whatever that situation may have been, Marie's husband was prospering. The son of a former Lord Provost of Edinburgh, Clerk would himself attain that position three times, from 1619-20, 1623-5 and 1630-4.[11] During the mid-1630s and probably before then, he owned a large house and yard just behind the place where the Tron Kirk now stands[12] and it was in 1623 that a seat for Marie 'the Provost's wife', was constructed in St Giles', almost certainly in the East Kirk. The following year her seat was re-formed, then in 1631-2 a seat was put up for her in the

Auld Kirk. That would have been in anticipation of Charles I's visit in 1633, when her husband would be sitting in the Provost's Loft and she too would expect to have a prominent position near the Royal Loft.[13] Clerk was knighted by Charles I during the King's Edinburgh visit and that same he year acquired the attractive estate of Pittencrieff, in Dunfermline. It was he who built Pittencrieff House which survives to this day, featuring his carved coat of arms and initials.[14]

Marie died on 2 June 1637, leaving silverwork worth £108, along with 500 merks of ready money, clothing, utensils and furnishings in the houses in Edinburgh, Pittencrieff and Stenton. The total value, with debts owed to her, came to over to £2200.[15] Her husband died on 2 September 1643 'of two days' sickness' and was interred in Gilbert Primrose's tomb, where Marie herself would have been buried.[16]

---

[1] Iain MacLaren, 'A Brief History of the Royal College of Surgeons of Edinburgh' in Res Medica, Journal of the Royal Medical Society, cclxviii, issue 2 (Edinburgh 2005), 55
[2] Charles G.D. Littleton, 'Primrose, Gilbert', ODNB (Oxford University Press, 2004) [Marie's brother]
[3] Scots Peerage, iii, 318
[4] Ibid., Roll of Edinburgh Burgesses and Guild Brethren 1406-1700 ed. Charles Boog Watson (Scottish Record Society 1929), 109
[5] MacLaren, op. cit., 55
[6] NRS, Wills and Testaments, Edinburgh Commissary Court, CC8/8/49/164-69 (Gilbert Primrose)
[7] MacLaren, op. cit. 55
[8] NRS, Wills and Testaments, Edinburgh Commissary Court, CC8/8/49/157-9 (Alison Graham)
[9] R. Monteith, An Theater of Mortality (Edinburgh 1704), 30
[10] NRS, Wills and Testaments, Edinburgh Commissary Court, CC8/8/49/164-69 (Gilbert Primrose)
[11] Lord Provosts of Edinburgh, 34-5

[12] *Edinburgh Housemail Taxation Book,* 338, 378, 379

[13] ECA, MS Dean of Guild Accounts 1568-1626, 1622-2, p.13; 1623-4, p.11; 1631, n/p

[14] *The Register of the Great Seal of Scotland 1620-1633* ed. John Maitland Thomson (Edinburgh 1894), vii, p.726, no. 2141; David Perry, 'Dunfermline, from "Saracen" castle to "populous manufacturing royal burrow" ' in *Proceedings of the Society of Antiquaries of Scotland* (1999), 807

[15] NRS, Wills and Testaments, Edinburgh Commissary Court, CC8/8/58/689-90 (Marie Primrose)

[16] *A Diary of the Public Correspondence of Sir Thomas Hope of Craighall, Bart.* (Bannatyne Club 1843), 195-6

# 22

## *Margaret Hamilton, Lady Acheson*

Margaret Hamilton, born in about 1602, came from an unusual background with strong Irish and continental connections. Her father was Sir John Hamilton, younger brother of the Roman Catholic 1st Earl of Abercorn who possessed extensive lands in Ireland, while her mother was the Flemish Johanna Everard, daughter of Levinus Everard, Councillor of State to the King of Spain in the province of Mechlin.[1] Margaret's father died some time before 1604, when she was still an infant, and her mother rapidly re-married, supplying her with the first of no fewer than three successive stepfathers. Johanna's new husband was Robert, 4th Lord Sempill, who had been Ambassador to Spain in 1596. Johanna herself would have been a Roman Catholic, and three years after their marriage, Sempill was excommunicated by the Church of Scotland as 'a confirmed and obstinate papist.' His estates were in the Paisley area, and Margaret would have spent her childhood there, the household now having the addition of her small half-brother, William Sempill.[2]

Lord Sempill died in 1611. Once again Johanna lost no time in finding a new husband, that very same year. Margaret's second stepfather was a Scot, Captain Patrick Crauford, who had been granted substantial lands in Letterkenny, Donegal, as part of the Plantation of Ulster, the scheme whereby Scottish and English Protestants were assigned property formerly owned by Irish Catholics. Crauford had already begun to develop Letterkenny into a prosperous market town and Margaret and her half-brother moved with their mother to live there. However, Crauford died within months of his marriage during a visit home to Scotland[3], whereupon the enterprising Johanna promptly married her fourth husband, Sir George Marbury, a gentleman from Lincolnshire who had been knighted by James VI and I in 1605.[4] No doubt at her urging, he was given the task of further developing Letterkenny, which to this day celebrates him as its founder, and in 1625 he built a castle there.[5]

Three years earlier, a marriage contract had been signed at Letterkenny between Margaret and Sir Archibald Acheson.[6] A Protestant Scotsman from East Lothian and a widower with several children, Acheson was a very successful advocate, and he too had an Irish connection. In 1611 he had received a large grant of land in Armagh, followed the next year by additional property in Cavan. After that, he divided his time between Ireland and Scotland, where he became an Extraordinary Lord of Session in 1628 and was made a baronet of Nova Scotia. At the same time, he was granted the influential position of one of the two Secretaries of State for Scotland.[7] It was obvious that he would now have to concentrate on his work in Edinburgh and in that same year a seat in St Giles' was set up for Margaret, probably in the East Kirk, by David Brown the wright and his three men. The work took them two and a half days, and cost the Dean of Guild of £4:13:4. Three months later Margaret had to vacate it temporarily, when the whole interior of St Giles' was about to be white-washed again. A ship's sail was borrowed from Leith to protect the carved and gilded King's Seat, scaffolding was brought in and twelve workmen moved all the seats and forms into a specially prepared room.[8] In 1631-2 another seat for 'Sir Archibald Acheson's lady' was being put up in St Giles', probably in the Auld Kirk in contemplation of Charles I's intended visit.[9]

By then, Margaret had a son, George, born in 1629,[10] and Acheson was building a handsome family house in Edinburgh's Canongate, at the foot of Bakehouse Close. Acheson House, today the headquarters of Edinburgh World Heritage, was completed in 1633. It bears above one of the windows his carved initials and over the next window those of 'DMH', Dame Margaret Hamilton.[11] Acheson was still going back and forward to Letterkenny, but the following year he died there of 'a pestilential fever.'[12] Margaret would not attend services in St Giles' again, for she 'turned Papist after Sir Archibald's death and said she had ventured her soul for an Acheson', according to Scot of Scotstarvet. This would seem to bear out the assumption that she had originally been brought up as a Catholic.[13] Acheson House passed to her husband's eldest son by his first marriage,[14] and Margaret and her small son George very likely went back to her mother's home in Letterkenny.[15] Johanna lived on until 14 June 1638,[16] but Margaret's date of death is unknown.

---

[1] *Scots Peerage*, i, 40

[2] *Scots Peerage*, vii, 551-552

[3] Patrick C. Coulson, *The Early Life of Erasmus O'Rourke* (Finedon 2009), 181

[4] *Scots Peerage*, vii, 551-552; John Nichols, *The Progresses, Processions and Magnificent Festivities of King James the First*, ii, (London 1828), ii, 48

[5] Coulson, op. cit., 181

[6] *Scots Peerage*, i, 40; ix, p.8, no. 40

[7] Brunton, *Lords of Session*, 224-225; *The Historical Works of Sir James Balfour*, ii, 48; *Handbook of British Chronology*, 187

[8] ECA, MS Dean of Guild Accounts 1626-1720, 6 May 1628, July 1628 n/p

[9] Ibid., 1631-1632, n/p

[10] Scot of Scotstarvet, op. cit., 77

[11] https://canmore.org.uk/site/52525

[12] Scot of Scotstarvet, 77; George Hill, *An Historical Account of the Plantation of Ulster at the Commencement of the Seventeenth Century 1608-1620* (Belfast 1877), 472

[13] Scot of Scotstarvet, 77

[14] https://canmore.org.uk/site/52525; NRS, Wills and Testaments, Edinburgh Commissary Court, CC8/8/57/170-172 (Archibald Acheson)

[15] *Scots Peerage*, vii, 554

[16] Ibid.; G[eorge] E[dward] C[okayne], *The Complete Baronetage 1625-1649* (Exeter 1903), ii, 355; *Scots Peerage*, i, 40

# 23

## *Margaret Craig, Lady Durie*

Margaret Craig spent her life in legal circles. Her father was the famous Thomas Craig of Riccarton, one of Edinburgh's leading advocates and the author of a celebrated work on feudal law. Margaret was his eldest daughter by his second wife Helen Heriot, and she was probably born around 1580. She would have been brought up in the large house that he built for himself in 1582 at the head of what was, as a result, named Craig's Close and later became part of the present day Cockburn Street. The family would have worshipped in St Giles'.[1]

In January 1596 Margaret married a promising young lawyer named Alexander Gibson, at that time Third Clerk of the Session. She then had three sons, Alexander, John and George, two of whom grew up to be successful advocates, and two daughters, Elizabeth and Margaret.[2] They lived at first near Edinburgh, in Wester Granton, where her husband owned a property, but in 1614, as his career progressed, he purchased the lands of Durie in the parish of Scoonie, seven miles north of Leven.[3] This became their country home, and he and Margaret continued to acquire further lands in Fife.[4] Her husband was an enthusiastic Presbyterian, to the extent that James VI on one occasion threatened to hang him because of his support for Robert Bruce the minister. He was an elder of Scoonie Church and became a committed supporter of the Covenanters.[5]

Much of the family's time, however, had to be spent in Edinburgh as Gibson had become a Lord of Session in 1621, choosing the title of Lord Durie. He was widely admired as 'a man of a penetrating wit and clear judgment, polished and improved by much study and exercise'.[6] By the early 1630s he owned a large house on the site of the Old Assembly Rooms in what became known as Durie's Close.[7] In addition, he leased out a stable there and rented a back chamber and two upstairs front chambers on the opposite side of the Lawnmarket. They were probably where he conducted his legal business.[8] By then, Margaret had been granted her own seat in St Giles'. There is no mention of it being built, but an iron bolt was added to it in 1629-30.[9] She had various relatives who were members of the congregation, including her nephew Archibald Johnston of Warriston, joint author of the National Covenant and son of her sister, Elizabeth.[10]

At about that same time, Durie's activities in the Court of Session resulted in an alarming episode which obviously caused Margaret great anxiety. A substantial lawsuit involving the Earl of Traquair was being heard before him, and it was rumoured that when it became obvious that Durie would find against Traquair, the Earl or someone acting on his behalf devised a plan to remove him as the judge. One Saturday afternoon when he was out on Leith Links 'at his diversion', Durie was attacked and kidnapped by strong masked men, who carried him off and shut him up in a windowless room somewhere in the country. There he was kept for three months and treated well, but no one knew what had happened to him. As the weeks went by, Margaret decided that he must be dead. She and the children accordingly put on mourning clothes for him. However, when the case which he had been prevented from hearing was finally concluded, Lord Durie was 'carried back by Incognitos and dropped in the same place where he had been taken up.' Almost incredibly, he had previously been kidnapped in 1604 for a similar reason, although the details of that incident have not been recorded.[11]

From 1642-3 Durie was Lord President of the Court of Session, but he died at his house of Durie on 10 June 1644 and was buried at Scoonie Church[12]. Margaret outlived him by thirteen years. On 24 July 1657, Mr John Lamont of Newton recorded in his diary that 'the old Lady Durie, in Fife, departed out of this life at Durie, about four o'clock in the afternoon and was interred at Scoonie Church the 31 of July.'[13]

---

[1] John W. Cairns, 'Craig, Thomas', *ODNB* (Oxford University Press, 2004); NRS, Wills and Testaments, Edinburgh Commissary Court, CC8/8/45/237-240 (Thomas Craig); Charles B. Boog Watson, 'Notes of the Closes and Wynds of Old Edinburgh' in *The Book of the Old Edinburgh Club*, xii (Edinburgh 1923), 27, 70

[2] Vaughan T. Wells, 'Alexander Gibson, Lord Durie', *ODNB* (Oxford University Press 2004-16); William Forbes, *A Journal of the Session Containing the Decisions of the Lords of Council and Session* (Edinburgh 1714), xxviii

[3] Wells, 'Alexander Gibson, Lord Durie', *ODNB* (Oxford University Press 2004)

[4] *The Register of the Great Seal, 1609-1620,* ed. John Maitland Thomson (Edinburgh 1892), vol vii, 476 no. 1305, 570-1 no. 1583; 691-2 no. 1910; 781-2 no. 2151

[5] Wells, 'Alexander Gibson, Lord Durie', *ODNB* (Oxford University Press 2004)

[6] Forbes, op. cit., xxviii

[7] Boog Watson, op. cit., 70

[8] *Edinburgh Housemails Taxation Book,* 115, 117, 437, 441, 443, 581

[9] ECA, MS Dean of Guild Accounts 1626-1720, n/p

[10] Cairns, 'Thomas Craig', *ODNB* (Oxford University Press 2004)

[11] Forbes, op. cit., 28

[12] *A Diary of the Public Correspondence of Sir Thomas Hope of Craighall, Bart, 1632-1645* (Bannatyne Club), 207-8

[13] *The Diary of Mr John Lamont of Newton 1649-1671* (Maitland Club 1830), 99

# 24

## *Margaret Ker, Lady Yester*

Margaret Ker is the most unusual member of this group of late sixteenth- and early seventeenth-century women, for she was not granted her seat in St Giles' because of her husband's status. Instead, it was a tribute to her own philanthropic activities, as the burgh records of Edinburgh of 1629-30 make clear. She had been twice widowed by then, and now it was noted that 'because of her pious disposition and charitable works, especially to the poor', Lady Yester had been granted the west part of the pew that she usually occupied.[1]

The impressively large house she had built for herself, with two cellars and both a front and a back entrance, was in the Auld Kirk parish, which stretched from just west of where the Tron Kirk now stands to the slope leading down to the Cowgate. She also rented a coach house on the south side of the Canongate.[2] Her seat was therefore in the Auld Kirk, directly in front of the pillar south of the pulpit. At the same time she was now also granted the little seat at the west entrance to her main one, where her attendants would sit.[3]

Born in about 1572, Margaret had originally come from a Borders family but her father, Mark Ker, was an Extraordinary Lord of Session and a constant attender of the Privy Council in Edinburgh. Towards the end of his life he was created 1st Earl of Lothian. When he died on 8 April 1609 he left the very large sum of almost £39,000, and in his Will he gave his blessing to his wife and children, praying that they would always fear and serve God. Margaret's mother and namesake, Margaret Maxwell, a daughter of Lady Herries, was still alive at that time.[4]

Margaret Ker was already married when her father died, having become the wife of James, 7th Lord Hay of Yester in May 1592, when she was about twenty. He had inherited his title the previous year. They lived near Gifford in East Lothian, at Yester (at that time known as Bothans) in the sixteenth-century tower house which had replaced the medieval castle owned by her husband's ancestors. Bothans Place, as he called their house, has since given way to the present day Yester House on the same site.[5] Margaret and her husband had four children, John, William, Robert and Margaret **(15)**,[6] and she is credited with having, 'by her wise and virtuous government', preserved and improved their lands.[7]

When at home the family attended the nearby St Bothans Church (now known as Yester Chapel) and indeed, Margaret and her husband were its principal proprietors. They had received a grant of its pre-Reformation ecclesiastical lands, and in 1606 Yester was quarrelling over who had the right to erect seats in its south aisle.[8] His main occupation was as Sheriff of Peebles and, being of an argumentative disposition, he was constantly involved in disputes with tenants and neighbours. He died in 1609, leaving almost £14,000, but debts of £8712:13:4. Margaret, 'my loving spouse', was to be his only executor 'as she will answer to God' and guardian of their under-age children. Had she died before him, then his friend Sir Andrew Ker of Ferniehirst would have taken on that role.[9]

Margaret remained a widow until 1614 when, at the age of about forty-two, she married Andrew, the son and heir of none other than Sir Andrew Ker of Ferniehirst.[10] He was about ten years younger. Margaret's new father-in-law was created 1st Lord Jedburgh in 1622 at her request, which would imply that she had considerable influence with James VI and I.[11] As a result, her second husband was known after that as the Master of Jedburgh but Margaret was allowed to retain her title and status as Lady Yester. The year before he had married her, the Master had been given the keepership of Dumfries Castle. Five years later, he became Captain of the Guard to James VI and a member of the Scottish Privy Council.[12] Margaret was much wealthier than he was and she is said to have created parks, gardens and buildings on his lands too, at her own expense.[13] He never did inherit his father's title and estates because he died before him, in 1629, just a year after being made an Extraordinary Lord of Session.[14]

Margaret's charitable activities were well-established by then. She was particularly active in erecting schools and hospitals, and in 1638 she financed the building and maintenance of a school (with schoolmaster) in Oxnam, near Jedburgh, and four little dwelling houses there for poor people 'in all time coming'.[15] When collections were made for the Tron Kirk which was being built in Edinburgh in the late 1630s, she subscribed £666:13:4 towards its costs.[16] Moreover, in 1644 she gave the sum of 10,000 merks to build a new church on the west side of High School Wynd in Edinburgh, the town's population having risen so much that the churches in St Giles' were vastly overcrowded. This was called Lady Yester's Church, for when her original donation proved to be insufficient, she assigned 1000 merks a year until it was completed. The Town Council then created a new parish for Lady Yester's Church, with 2,181 parishioners.[17]

Margaret died on 15 March 1647 at the age of seventy-four. She was buried in a special aisle in her church and her monument with its gilded skull and crossbones bears her epitaph in Latin. Its last two lines translate as 'Let it be the care of all who live hereafter, To live and die like Margaret, Lady Yester'.[18] Her church was united with Greyfriars Kirk in 1938, but her original gilded memorial with the epitaph is now displayed in the Lady Yester Aisle there.[19] (Plate 6)

[1] *Edinburgh Burgh Extracts 1642-1655*, 25-26

[2] *Edinburgh Housemails Taxation Book*, 259; Dugald Butler, *The Tron Kirk of Edinburgh* (Edinburgh 1906), 44

[3] *Edinburgh Burgh Extracts 1642-1655*, 25-26

[4] *Scots Peerage*, v, 455-458; NRS, Wills and Testaments, Edinburgh Commissary Court, CC8/8/46/298-307 (Mark Ker)

[5] https://canmore.org.uk/site/56062/yester-castle-and-goblin-ha

[6] *Scots Peerage*, viii, 446-447

[7] Daniel Wilson, *Memorials of Edinburgh in the Olden Time* (Edinburgh 1872), 429

[8] *Scots Peerage*, viii, 445

[9] *Scots Peerage*, viii, 445; NRS, Wills and Testaments, Edinburgh Commissary Court, CC8/8/46/109-120 (James Hay of Yester)

[10] NRS, Leven and Melville Papers, GD26/6/29, minute of marriage contract, 1614

[11] Wilson, op. cit., 429

[12] *Scots Peerage*, v, 75-6

[13] Wilson, op. cit., 429

[14] *Scots Peerage*, v, 75-76; Brunton, *Lords of Session*, 279

[15] NRS, Lothian Muniments, GD40/3/408, Extract mortification by Lady Yester; NRS Papers of the Maule Family, Earls of Dalhousie, GD45/26/18, List of Mortifications by Lady Yester

[16] Butler, op. cit., 132

[17] William Maitland, *The History of Edinburgh from its foundation to the Present Time* (Edinburgh 1753, ECCO print edition), 181

[18] Ibid., 182; R. Monteith, *An Theater of Mortality* (Edinburgh 1704), 51

[19] A. Ian Dunlop, *The Kirks of Edinburgh 1560-1984* (Scottish Record Society 1989), 88-91

# 25

## *Katherine Carnegie, Countess of Traquair*

Katherine Carnegie's life demonstrates the domestic repercussions of the bitter struggle between those Scots who supported the National Covenant and their opponents. Her parents were both from Angus families. Her father was David Carnegie of Kinnaird, later 1st Earl of Southesk and her mother was Margaret Lindsay of Edzell. They had ten children, Katherine being the third of their six daughters. She was probably born in about 1605, and her early years would have been spent at the medieval Kinnaird Castle near Brechin, which was the family's principal residence. A staunch supporter of Charles I's determination to keep bishops in the Church of Scotland as part of the royal policy of bringing it into line with the Church of England, her father refused to sign the National Covenant in 1638, but later agreed, after a brief spell of imprisonment by the Covenanters.[1]

By that time Katherine had long since been married, for her contract was signed on 14 September 1620. Her husband was Sir John Stewart of Traquair, and she brought him a tocher of 20,000 merks, a handsome sum for a younger daughter. Their only son, John, was born two years later, and they also had four daughters, Margaret, Elizabeth, Katherine and Magdalene. Stewart's financial expertise won him the favour of Charles I. The King created him Earl of Traquair in 1633 and made him Lord High Treasurer three years later. His portrait by an unknown artist shows him with a seemingly diffident air despite the grandeur of his robes. However, although he was praised by his contemporaries for his learning and his financial acumen, he was trusted by neither side in the religious conflict, being widely disliked as a crafty, unreliable bully.[2]

Traquair House was the family's principal home, but he also had a house in Niddry's Wynd, Edinburgh and property in Linton, Roxburghshire.[3] Unusually, it seems that he and Katherine occupied the same seat in St Giles', for in 1630 David Brown the wright, his two men and two boys had been paid a day's wage of £3:10/- for setting up 'Lord and Lady Traquair's seat'.[4] Known to be a friend of Archbishop Laud, Katherine's husband was in 1637 widely believed to have been behind the attempt to impose the English style prayer book on Scotland and was even rumoured to have Roman Catholic sympathies. However, others were convinced that it was he who had organised the so-called Jenny Geddes riot in St Giles' against the prayer book. His attempts to reconcile the two opposing sides came to nothing, and by 1644 the General Assembly were declaring him to be an enemy of religion. He and his son, usually on very bad terms, fought together in the royalist army at the Battle of Preston in 1648, where he was captured and subsequently imprisoned in Warwick Castle for four years.[5]

Despite Traquair's now ruined reputation and the fact that his estates were burdened with enormous debts, Katherine's letters to him at that time show her to have been a devoted wife, although the present-day reader may suspect that she too may have long been the victim of his domineering nature. Only six of her letters have been preserved, dating from 1651, but they are lengthy, anxious and explanatory. Writing from Edinburgh, she always addresses him in the terminology of the time as 'My

Dearest Heart', signing herself 'Your truly loving wife and humble servant'. She describes her desperate and unsuccessful attempts to contact the friends whom he thought would support him and agitate for his release, but unfortunately for some reason she had lost most of the power in her right foot, with the result that she could not go anywhere herself to speak to potential allies.

Instead, she wrote to the influential people her husband suggested, asking them to visit her, but they did not come. Others promised much but did nothing. She frequently asked her father for advice, but he was very wary of involving himself after his own previous experiences. Her brother Lord Carnegie was her husband's bitter enemy, she said, and under his influence although her son John was always promising to help, he did nothing. His lack of cooperation was ascribed to the belief that his father had consistently bullied him. Indeed, Katherine advised her husband 'to write fair and kindly to him', for that would mean more to John than anything anyone else said to him. Unfortunately, the letters her husband sent to people himself were misinterpreted and, she said, 'they are like to go mad at me' when she justified what he had written. 'I may err in judgment', she concluded, 'but while I breathe I shall be faithful to you and ever witness how much I am your truly loving wife and servant.'[6]

Oliver Cromwell allowed her husband to return to Scotland the following year. Financially ruined, he had to sell his houses at both Traquair and Linton in 1656 and 1657. He was even rumoured to have died begging in the streets of Edinburgh, but that was untrue, for he died at home, on 27 March 1659. There is no record of whether Katherine was still alive by then.[7]

[1] *Scots Peerage*, viii, 64-68; MacDonald, A., 'Carnegie, David, first earl of Southesk nobleman', *ODNB* (Oxford University Press 2004), Brunton, *Lords of Session*, 258-259

[2] *Scots Peerage*, viii, 402-405; J.R.M. Sizer, 'Stewart, John, first earl of Traquair', *ODNB* (Oxford University Press 2004). (Includes colour image of his portrait by an unknown artist, in the collection of Traquair House Charitable Trust)

[3] John A. Inglis, 'Sir John Hay, 'The Incendiary', in *Book of the Old Edinburgh Club*, no. 57 (October 1917), 138

[4] ECA, MS Dean of Guild Accounts, 1626-1720, 1630-31, n/p

[5] *Scots Peerage*, viii, 402-405; Sizer, 'John Stewart, first earl of Traquair', *ODNB* (Oxford University Press 2004)

[6] William Fraser, *History of the Carnegies, Earls of Southesk and their Kindred*, (Edinburgh 1867), ii, 441-447

[7] *Scots Peerage*, viii, 404-405; Sizer, 'Stewart, John, first earl of Traquair', *ODNB* (Oxford University Press 2004)

# 26

## *Elizabeth Bennet, Lady Hope*

Elizabeth Bennet was the daughter of Robert Bennet, Town Clerk of Musselburgh and his wife Euphame Seton, a distant relative of the Earls of Winton.[1] Her date of birth is unknown, but by 1602 she was the wife of twenty-nine-year-old Thomas Hope, who came from an Edinburgh merchant family.[2] His legal career was going from strength to strength and from 1628 he occupied the position of sole Lord Advocate, an office which he had shared with a colleague who died that year. At the same time, he became a member of the Scottish Privy Council and a baronet of Nova Scotia.[3] It was in 1630-31 that David Brown the wright with his men and two boys put up Elizabeth's seat in the Auld Kirk of St Giles'.[4]

By then, her family was complete. She had given birth to at least fourteen children but in that age of high child mortality, death had taken its sad toll. Her first baby, born in 1603 and named after herself, did not survive. William, Henry, David, Patrick and her last child Charles, born in 1627, all died in infancy or early childhood, as did Margaret, her second daughter. Fortunately John, Thomas, Alexander, James, Mary, another Elizabeth and Anne reached adult life, but four of them predeceased their mother.[5] It used to be said that because families were so large in those days, parents did not grieve when they lost a child, but research into surviving Early Modern correspondence shows that this was far from being so.[6]

Elizabeth's husband had originally lived in the Cramond area and had been a member of Cramond Church, where he gifted a new aisle on the north side of the building in the early 1630s.[7] However, by then he had acquired various properties elsewhere. The family home was now an imposing mansion in Niddry's Wynd, on the west side of St Giles', and he rented an equally handsome upper house close to it. He also had Craighall Castle, on the estate that he had purchased in Fife.[8] He used Craighall with increasing frequency, Elizabeth often joining him a few days later with 'the family', meaning several of their children, grandchildren and probably some additional servants.[9]

Family relationships meant a great deal to both him and Elizabeth, as his diary shows. As soon as their sons married, he was referring warmly to their wives as 'my daughter Helen', 'my daughter Anne' and so forth, and Elizabeth was often to be found in the company of her grandchildren, attending their births, as was the custom, and helping to care for them when they fell ill. On one occasion in 1641, she had a brisk argument with her husband. Her daughter-in-law Anne Foulis, wife of their son James, gave birth to a little boy on 6 November, but the baby was so weak that Hope wanted him to be baptised right away. Elizabeth refused to arrange this, saying that because of the infant's fragility, they did not dare take him to the church in the cold November weather. Hope brushed this aside, recording in his diary that he had the child baptised in the nearby Magdalen Chapel, but the baby died on the evening of 7 November, 'And my wife was angry at my grief'. Did that mean that Elizabeth had managed to reconcile herself to the loss of so many of her own children and grandchildren with the thought that they were safe in the arms of the Lord? That is probable, for it was the conventional belief, but her personal experience of child mortality was obviously still very painful.[10]

Normally, she and her husband were united in their attitude to family business. In 1637, when their 26-year-old son Alexander was pursuing his career in London, his parents were furious when he borrowed the large sum of £70 sterling and asked his father to pay the debt for him. Hope sent him 'a very angry letter, and his mother another'. Elizabeth wrote regularly to her sons when they were away in London or abroad, and this was not the first time that she had complained to Alexander about his spending. She was also in the habit of sending him provisions, on one occasion enclosing a note of the oats, cheese, salmon and herring that she had sent him.[11]

Sometimes she hired her husband's servants for him, in 1644 appointing John Clerk to replace the boy who had been attending him and she took letters from Hope at Craighall to deliver in Edinburgh on the occasions when she was going to be there before him. Amidst the disturbances of the 1640s she carried a packet of documents to the Earl of Panmure when she went to the capital 'to close up the vaults and to sand the upmost [upper] house, for fear of grenades'. The Covenanters were at that point planning to besiege Edinburgh Castle, and Niddry's Wynd would be in the line of fire.[12]

Now that she and her husband were living so close to St Giles', they were members of the congregation, but in 1637 he received a letter from William Laud, Archbishop of Canterbury, reproaching him for having taken Communion at Pencaitland, presumably because Hope was unhappy that St Giles' had become a Cathedral with its own bishop in 1633.[13] In August 1639 he would note in his diary that the General Assembly of the Church of Scotland had declared episcopacy to be unlawful, 'to the unspeakable joy of all them that fears the Lord.'[14] In May 1641 he was back at Cramond, taking Communion there, but the following year, however, he attended Communion in the East Kirk of St Giles' once more.[15]

He was by then deeply dismayed, his support for the Covenanters conflicting painfully with his allegiance to Charles I. This famously resulted in him having a number of disturbing dreams, which seemed to him to carry symbolic messages. We have no direct evidence of Elizabeth's views, but she was his supportive confidante. In April 1639 he awoke one day to hear a voice saying to him 'I will preserve and save my people'. He asked Elizabeth if she had heard anyone speaking, but she had not, and so he told her what the voice had said. Unfortunately his diary does not record her response. In October 1643, he dreamed that he lost three ordinary gold pieces and a large one, and was told that he would find the three smaller coins but not the big one. In the dream, he asked Elizabeth what this could mean, but in reality he told no one, because she was away at the time, attending to yet another dying grandson.[16]

Hope eventually fell ill at their Edinburgh house on the night of Saturday 26 September 1646, his son James noting in his own diary that his father's condition worsened the following day and instead of going to church with the rest of the family, his mother stayed at home with her husband. Dr Alexander Kincaid and Dr Henry Purves the surgeon were summoned, but although he revived a little after their treatment and gave the family his blessing, Hope died during the evening of Thursday, 1 October 1646.[17] Elizabeth lived on until 1660 when she would probably have been in her late seventies. Her Testament reveals that she had been ill for two years, with the result that Dr Purves and other doctors were now claiming for their frequent visits and consultations during that time. Similarly, John Foulis and other unnamed apothecaries were owed £600 for her drugs and medicaments. She was buried in Greyfriars Churchyard on 12 February.[18] Her Testament was registered at Edinburgh Commissary Court on 8 February 1666 by Sir Alexander Hope, now her sole surviving son.[19]

---

[1] *Scots Peerage*, iv, 489; viii, 572n

[2] Archibald Stewart Denham, *The Coltness Collections: Memorials of the Stewarts of Allanton, Coltness and Goodtrees* (Maitland Club, Glasgow 1842), 16

[3] *Handbook of British Chronology*, 196; *Scot of Scotstarvet*, 109-10; 'Sir Thomas Hope of Craighall', *ODNB* (Oxford University Press 2004)

[4] ECA, Dean of Guild M.S. Accounts, 1626-1720, 1630-1631, n/p

[5] *Scots Peerage*, iv, 489-491

[6] Rosalind K. Marshall, *Childhood in Seventeenth-Century Scotland* (National Galleries of Scotland exhibition catalogue, Edinburgh 1976), 22-25; Rosalind K. Marshall, *Virgins and Viragos: A History of Women in Scotland from 1080-1980* (London and Chicago 1983), 121-122; Rosalind K. Marshall, 'Attitudes to death in seventeenth-century Scotland' in *The Nursing Mirror*, (London, 9 November 1983), xiii-xvi

[7] NRS, Papers of the Dukes of Buccleuch, GD224/170/15, Papers relating to repairs of the church of Cramond

[8] *Edinburgh Housemails Taxation Book*, 67; Daniel Wilson, *Memorials of Edinburgh in the Olden Time* (Edinburgh 1848), 177; https://canmore.org.uk/site/33017/craighall-castle

[9] *A Diary of the Public Correspondence of Sir Thomas Hope of Craighall, Bart, 1633-1645* (Bannatyne Club 1843), 116

[10] Ibid., 154

[11] Ibid., 62, 64, 69, 84

[12] Ibid., 116, 117 (2), 204

[13] Ibid., 61

[14] Ibid., 104

[15] Ibid., 136, 170, 171

[16] Ibid., 89, 197

[17] *The Diary of Sir James Hope 1646-1654* ed. James Balfour Paul, (*Miscellany of the Scottish History Society* 1919) series 2, vol. 19, 193-194

[18] *Register of Interments in the Greyfriars Burying Ground, Edinburgh, 1656-1700*, ed. Henry Paton (Scottish Record Society 1902), 51

[19] NRS, Wills and Testaments, Edinburgh Commissary Court, CC8/8/72/186-187 (Elizabeth Bennet)

# 27

## *Marie Sutton, Countess of Home*

Marie Sutton was one of the few members of the English nobility who married into the Scottish peerage in the early seventeenth century. Born on 2 October 1586, she was the eldest daughter of Edward Sutton, 9th Lord Dudley and his wife Theodosia Harington, who had married when Dudley was only fourteen. Marie's childhood circumstances were difficult. Her father had inherited numerous debts from his father and to make matters worse he abandoned his wife and children in London, 'without provision and sustenance' and went to live with a collier's daughter in Dudley, with whom he had numerous sons and daughters. When Marie was ten, her mother successfully sued her husband for maintenance for herself and their children, but despite warnings from the English Privy Council he soon fell into arrears with the payments.[1]

Marie's prospects did not look good, but one of James VI's policies in pursuit of his desire to bring his two kingdoms of Scotland and England even closer together was to encourage the intermarriage of Scottish and English peers. It was probably he who suggested that Dudley could improve his financial position by marrying his eldest daughter to the very wealthy Scotsman, Alexander, Lord Home. The wedding took place on 11 July 1605, just four months after James had created the bridegroom 1st Earl of Home, and Marie's circumstances were transformed. She was now eighteen and a countess. Her husband was a Roman Catholic widower twenty years older than she was and, like others among his contemporaries, he had married a Protestant wife in an attempt to protect his public career from criticism. He had no children by that first marriage and now that he was a peer, he would have been particularly anxious to have a son and heir.[2]

Marie's marriage to him seems to have been a happy one, and together they had two sons, James and William, two daughters, Margaret and Anne, and another child who did not survive, all born with the help of Mrs Cuthbert, a midwife Marie summoned from England[3]. Despite his marriage, Home remained in constant trouble with the Church of Scotland because of his Catholicism, and had to withdraw to the continent from time to time as a result, but he was protected by the King and made impressive progress in his official role of pacifying the Borders. Fourteen years after their marriage, Marie and he went to London to attend the funeral of the Queen, Anne of Denmark, but her husband died during their visit, on 5 April 1619. Marie brought his body back to Scotland for burial in the Home family vault in Dunglass Church.[4] Their children were still minors, of course, and in his Will he had made her his sole executor and guardian of their two daughters.[5] So was she the 'Lady Home' who in 1631-2 was granted her own seat in St Giles' during the rush to have a significant position during Charles I's expected visit in 1633?[6] After the death of her husband, the documents of the time continue to refer to her as 'Countess of Home' or 'Lady Home' rather than 'Dowager Countess', which was not a term normally used in the Scotland of the time.[7]

As a wealthy widow, Marie divided her time between her properties in Scotland and London. Her main Scottish home during her widowhood was what is now known as Moray House, in the Canongate. This she built or more probably rebuilt in 1618. With its fashionable plaster ceilings and its expensive furnishings, many of them acquired in London, it would become even more famous for the beautiful terraced gardens that she laid out.[8] She also had a liferent of the lands of Dunglass, about a mile from Cockburnspath in East Lothian. Not to be confused with Dunglass in Dunbartonshire, her castle stood on the main road to England and her husband had entertained James VI there when he set off for London in 1603.

On 17 August 1641, however, Marie was complaining to the Scottish parliament that the building had been almost completely destroyed the previous year by a devastating explosion. She had not been there at the time, for Thomas, 2nd Earl of Haddington had been holding the castle for the Covenanters. The cause of this notorious explosion has never been fully explained, but it is thought to have been caused, perhaps deliberately, by gunpowder stored in the castle cellars. Not only was Haddington among those who were killed, but practically the whole building had been destroyed, along with all Marie's fashionable furnishings, gardens and plantings. She was therefore claiming over £40,000, which would allow her to restore the small part of the house which had not been completely ruined, and her son, who was now 2nd Earl of Home, was subsequently paid the compensation.[9]

Marie's London home was a large house in Aldersgate Street, a spacious street of handsome mansions. At its north end was the imposing archway commemorating the fact that James VI had passed through it when he arrived from Scotland in 1603. Originally built in 1582 by Sir Richard Martin, Lord Mayor of London, Marie's house has now been painted white and is an arts and education centre, its extensive grounds forming part of Waterlow Park.[10] She

DISCOVERED LIVES

died there on 24 May 1645, leaving her Edinburgh house to her daughter Margaret, who had married James, 5th Earl of Moray, and her London home to her other daughter Anne, wife of John, later 1st Duke of Lauderdale, hence the modern names of these two properties.[11]

[1] http://www.historyofparliamentonline.org.volume/1558-1603/member/dudley

[2] Robert Fairlie, *Neanica*, (Edinburgh 1628), sig. E1; *Scots Peerage*, iv, 463-465; M. Meikle, 'Home, Alexander, first earl of Home', *ODNB* (Oxford University Press 2004)

[3] Papers of the Earl of Moray, NRAS 217 box 5, no. 295, letter of Mary, Countess of Westmoreland to her daughter Grace Fane, Countess of Home, 1627-31

[4] *Scots Peerage*, iv, 465

[5] NRS, Wills and Testaments, Edinburgh Commissary Court, CC8/8/51/92-97 (Alexander Home)

[6] ECA, MS Dean of Guild Accounts 1626-1720, n/p

[7] e.g. *RPC*, iv, 1630-1632, 641; ibid., vii, 556; NRS, Papers of the Home-Robertson Family of Paxton, Berwickshire (Home of Wedderburn), GD267/26/17/363, 369

[8] https://www.ed.ac.uk/education/about-us/maps-estates-history/estates/history/history; Michael Pearce, 'Closet and Cabinet', https://vanishedcomforts.wordpress.com/2017/10/07/closet-and-cabinet

[9] The Records of the Parliament of Scotland to 1707: http://www.rps.ac.uk/search.php?action=print&id=18027&filename=charlesi_trans&type=trans

[10] Henry Benjamin Wheatley, *London Past and Present: Its History, Associations and Traditions* (Cambridge 1891), i, 22; *Survey of London, xvii, the Parish of St Pancras*, Part 1, *The Village of Highgate*, edd. Percy Lovell and William MB. Marcham (London 1936), 7-18; http://Lauderdalehouse.org.uk

[11] *Scots Peerage*, iv, 465

# 28

## *Elizabeth Wilson, Lady Wardlaw*

Elizabeth Wilson came from an Edinburgh family with strong links to St Giles'. We do not know her date of birth, but she was Lucas Wilson's youngest daughter.[1] Her father, a successful merchant burgess, was Dean of Guild from 1577 to 1580, and therefore responsible for the upkeep of the church building. In late 1579, for instance, the provost, bailies and town council were ordering him to buy six lamps 'for serving in the kirk in the winter tide'.[2] When he died in June 1589, at 'a great age', his Testament showed that he and his family had been living in a rented house in Little's Close, on the north side of the High Street. He did not mention his children in his Will, but his wife, Katherine Udward, was to be his executor, with the advice of his brother-in-law Alexander Udward, another prominent Edinburgh merchant burgess who was by then Dean of Guild.[3]

These connections must have made it a particularly proud day for Elizabeth when in 1631-32 the latest Dean of Guild gave instructions for a seat to be set up in St Giles' for her. That had nothing to do with her family history, of course, but was because she was 'Sir Henry Wardlaw's lady'.[4] Her marriage contract had been signed about forty years earlier, on 23 September 1592 and the wedding would have followed soon after that. Her bridegroom came from Balmule in Fife, about three miles north of Dunfermline, and had been baptised in nearby Dunfermline Abbey Church in 1565. He studied law at the College of Guyenne in Bordeaux, having been recommended by George Buchanan, the famous Reformer, as a diligent student and the descendant of 'a good family'. Returning to Scotland eight or nine years later, he had embarked on his career as a lawyer.[5]

Two years after his marriage to Elizabeth, Wardlaw was admitted as a burgess and guild brother of Edinburgh, by right of his wife, in other words because of her father's career.[6] She probably also brought him a handsome tocher, for they were able to purchase the mill of Balmule and its lands, and their coats of arms were carved on a stone above the stable door there.[7] While her husband's career advanced, Elizabeth had thirteen or fourteen children, including two sets of twins: Henry, James, William, John, George, James and his twin Katherine, Elizabeth and her twin Alexander, Rachel, Anna, Anna, Christian and possibly Dorothy. The first James had died and the death of the first Anna in 1606 had been a double disappointment, for she had been called after James VI's wife, Anne of Denmark, with whom Wardlaw had a special connection.[8]

The Queen had received the abbey lands of Dunfermline from the King, and she had not only had the abbey guest house reconstructed for herself, but she had built a handsome new palace nearby, where she presided over a sophisticated and elegant Court.[9] The significance of this for Elizabeth was that in 1602 her husband had been made Chamberlain to the Queen and in 1607, as a reward for his faithful administration in that position, he was created hereditary Chamberlain of the Lordship of Dunfermline.[10] When Elizabeth had another little girl in Edinburgh in 1608, she was promptly called Anna and baptised in Dunfermline.[11]

The property at Balmule was probably too small now for the Wardlaw household and in 1608, Elizabeth and her husband were able to purchase the nearby lands of Pitreavie which had Wardlaw connections and, incidentally, in the Middle Ages had belonged to one of the altars in St Giles'. Wardlaw built a handsome four-storey tower house in Balmule, large enough to accommodate his growing family and of course demonstrate his prestige. His carved initials featured on several of the walls, with Elizabeth's on the sundial in the garden.[12] In 1609, she became Lady Wardlaw when her husband was knighted.[13]

Of course his legal and important financial duties in the king's service meant that a good deal of their time was spent in Edinburgh. By the mid-1630s they had an impressively large house on the north side of the High Street, opposite St Giles', with a rented stable on the south side.[14] Wardlaw had obtained his seat in the East Kirk by 1613,[15] Elizabeth now had hers, and they were probably regular attenders. So what were their views in these years of ecclesiastical turmoil? Although on Easter Sunday 1622 there were 250 people at Communion in the Auld Kirk, a service which was also attended by members of the East Kirk, only eight were named as kneeling to receive the bread and the wine as they were supposed to do, in keeping with royal policy. One of them was Sir Henry Wardlaw. Elizabeth is not mentioned.[16]

As a loyal supporter of James VI and then Charles I, her husband was created a baronet in 1631. He was as busy as ever with public business but on 29 January 1636 he made his Will, declaring himself to be 'weak and diseased in my body'. His executors were to be 'my well beloved spouse' and their third son John. He made bequests to various organisations including the College of Edinburgh 'to buy books', to the widows in Dunfermline Hospital and to the distressed prisoners in Edinburgh Tolbooth. Elizabeth had the key to the private place in his study where he kept the money to be used for those bequests, and she was to distribute it in accordance with his stated instructions. He died in Edinburgh on 5 April 1637, leaving over £17,000. Elizabeth had the liferent of their house on the north side of the High Street, duly registered his Testament and handed over the charitable donations.[17] In 1616 Anne of Denmark had gifted Wardlaw a vault in Dunfermline Abbey for himself and his posterity, under the three east pillars on the south side of the church and he was buried there,[18] but when Elizabeth died in June 1643, although her death was registered in Dunfermline, she was buried in Edinburgh, perhaps with her parents or some of her children.[19]

---

[1]*Roll of Edinburgh Burgesses and Guild-Brethern 1406-1700*, ed. Charles B. Boog Watson (Scottish Record Society 1929), 115

[2] *Edinburgh Burgh Extracts 1573-1589*, 141

[3] NRS, Wills and Testaments, Edinburgh Commissary Court, CC8/8/22/578-80 (Lucas Wilson); *Edinburgh Burgh Extracts 1589-1603*, 6, 27, 48, 58, 71, 139, 162, 165

[4]ECA, Dean of Guild MS Accounts 1626-1720, n/p

[5] John C. Gibson, *The Wardlaws in Scotland* (Edinburgh 1912), 117

[6] *Roll of Edinburgh Burgesses*, 115

[7] Gibson, op. cit., 118

[8] Gibson, op. cit., 126-128

[9] Meikle, M., & Payne, 'Anne [Anna, Anne of Denmark] (1574–1619), queen of England, Scotland, and Ireland, consort of James VI and I', *ODNB* (Oxford University Press 2004)

[10] Gibson, op. cit., 119

[11] *Parish Registers of Dunfermline 1561-1700*, ed. Henry Paton (Scottish Record Society 1911), 117; Gibson, op. cit., 127

[12] J.M. Webster, *Lands of Dunfermline* ed. S. Pitcairn (www.royaldunfermline.com/Resources/lands_of_Dunfermline.pdf),

10-11; Gibson, op. cit., 119-120;
https://canmore.org.uk/site/51015/pitreavie-castle
[13] Gibson, op. cit., 120
[14] *Edinburgh Housemails Taxation Book*, 176, 382
[15]ECA, Dean of Guild MS Accounts 1626-1720, November 1613, n/p; *Edinburgh Burgh Extracts 1604-1626*, 108
[16] David Calderwood, *The History of the Kirk of Scotland* (Wodrow Society, 1845), vii, 546; *The Register of the Privy Council of Scotland 1619-1622, ed.* David Masson (Edinburgh 1895), 707n
[17] NRS, Wills and Testaments, Edinburgh Commissary Court, CC8/8/58/542-546 (Henry Wardlaw); *Edinburgh Burgh Extracts 1604-1626*, 190; Gibson, op. cit., 121
[18] Gibson, op. cit., 120
[19] Ibid., 126

# 29

## *Janet Johnston, Lady Curriehill*

Janet Johnston was the granddaughter of the very wealthy Sir John Arnot of Berswick, who had twice been Lord Provost of Edinburgh.[1] Her mother, Rachel Arnot, was famous as an energetic opponent of bishops in the Church of Scotland. Described in her Latin epitaph as 'a mother to true religion' whose mind was 'God-inspired', Rachel frequently held meetings of Covenanting ministers and supporters in her house in Sciennes, Edinburgh, and indeed, for a number of years she is said to have concealed there the deposed minister Robert Bruce.[2] Janet's father, Archibald Johnston, was another of those prosperous merchants who were known for their opposition to the Scottish ecclesiastical policies of James VI and Charles I.[3]

Janet, their only daughter, brought up in that household, was not surprisingly influenced by her parents' views. She first appears in the records when she was married on 7 December 1603 to James Skene, who had become an advocate five months earlier.[4] The son of Sir John Skene of Curriehill the eminent lawyer and his wife Helen Somerville **(5)**, he was made a Lord of Session in 1612, as Lord Curriehill. Fourteen years later he would rise to the position of Lord President of the Court of Session.[5] He owned a large house at the eastern part of High School Yards in Edinburgh[6] and, according to the Skene family history, which is not always accurate in its details, Janet and he had eight sons. Of those, only John and Thomas survived, along with their three sisters, Rachel, Euphemia and Helen.[7]

Characterised by a modern writer as one of Edinburgh's most formidable and powerful matrons,[8] Janet no doubt had an influence on her husband's religious views. As a supporter of the presbyterian form of church government, he found that, like other contemporaries occupying important public offices, his private convictions conflicted with his loyalty to the monarch's policies. In July 1619, for instance, he was called before the Scottish Privy Council for failing to obey James VI and I's orders to the Lords of Session to attend the Easter Sunday service at St Giles', kneeling to take Communion in keeping with the recent Five Articles of Perth. His enemies claimed that he had gone elsewhere and had not knelt, which is what many of the opponents of the Five Articles did. Indeed, there was much gossip at the time claiming that Skene's wife Janet, 'a religious gentlewoman' and his mother-in-law Rachel Arnot were responsible for his alleged absence, for they had kept him at home.

He, however, vigorously denied that there was any truth in the accusation, saying that he had been so busy from 2 p.m. until 6 p.m. on the previous afternoon, examining witnesses for a forthcoming trial which he was hearing, that he had no time to go to the required preparatory sermon. He therefore could not attend the Easter Communion and so he had stayed in his house that morning. However, he had gone to the afternoon service, as his fellow Lords of Session could bear witness. The Privy Council promptly wrote to the King, exonerating him. James VI replied that he was glad to hear it, but added that the accusations against Skene had been most convincing, coming as they did from a reliable quarter, and so in order to give full satisfaction he must attend a Communion service as soon as possible and kneel. He obviously complied, for that ended the matter.[9]

By the 1630s Janet was regularly giving advice to her nephew, the famous Archibald Johnston of Warriston, co-author of the National Covenant, who mentions her no fewer than fifteen times in his 1632-1639 diary. His parents were deeply religious and he had attended Communion in the churches in St Giles' from his teenage years onwards. He discussed his possible choice of bride with Janet, and she was no doubt at his first wedding in the Auld Kirk in 1632, to Jean Stewart, daughter of Margaret Winram **(32)**. When his young wife went into labour, he sent at once for Janet as well as for the well-known Dr Arnot. Sadly Jean died in childbirth, and later he had long, agonised discussions with Janet on how to deal with his inward sexual temptations, which she sensibly advised him to ignore rather than dwelling on them.[10] One Sunday, he mentions having sat weeping between sermons at the desk which formed part of her stall in St Giles'.[11] This was erected for her in 1631-1632, when the Dean of Guild's accounts mention that 'the Lady President's seat' had been put up at a cost of £6.[12]

Whatever degree of influence Janet had on her husband's ecclesiastical views, when he made his Will on 4 October 1633, he nominated their young children Thomas and Helen as his executors, but added that 'my loving spouse Dame Janet Johnston' should give up the inventory of his goods in their names (which she did). He also declared that their bairns must follow her advice and counsel and obey her in all things. The Will was witnessed by Janet's brother, Samuel Johnston, and by her nephew, Archibald Johnston of Warriston. Her husband died twelve days later at the age of 54 and, at his own wish, was buried in Greyfriars Church beside his parents' sepulchre.[13]

By 1637 Janet had married again, becoming the fourth wife of the wealthy James Inglis of Ingliston, whose estate lay just to the west of Edinburgh. He too was a supporter of the Covenanters and they had probably known each other for a long time. Their marriage was to be fairly brief, however, for he was one of those killed in the notorious explosion on 30 August 1640, at Dunglass Castle, owned by Marie, Countess of Home **(27)** and her son but at that time being held by the Covenanters. His eldest son, Alexander, was his executor, and in the Will which Inglis had made in January of that same year, he left instructions that he was to be buried in his family vault in Kirkliston Church beside his parents, wives and children. As to his current wife, Alexander was to pay Janet the sums of money due to her under the terms of her marriage contract. It is not known when she died, or if she then joined her husband and her predecessors in their family tomb.[14]

---

[1] *The Lord Provosts of Edinburgh*, 30; NRS, Wills and Testaments, Edinburgh Commissary Court, CC8/8/49/175-179 (John Arnot)

[2] Jamie Reid Baxter, 'Posthumous Preaching: James Melville's Ghostly Advice in Ane Dialogue (1619), with an Edition from the Manuscript' in *Studies in Scottish Literature*, (South Carolina 2017), xxxxiii, 1, 83; Gilbert Burnet, *Bishop Burnet's History of His Own Time* (London 1724), i, 18

[3] James Johnston Brown, 'The Social, Political and Economic Influences of the Edinburgh Merchant Elite, 1600-1638', (Doctoral Thesis, Edinburgh University 1986), ii, 484

[4] W. F. Skene, *Memorials of the Family of Skene of Skene* (New Spalding Club 1887), 114; *The Register of Marriages for the Parish of Edinburgh 1595-1700*, ed. Henry Paton (Scottish Record Society 1908), 631

[5] Brunton, *Lords of Session*, 253-254

[6] *Edinburgh Housemails Taxation Book*, 426

[7] Skene, op. cit., 114 has confused the parentage of Archibald Johnston's wife Rachel with that of her niece, but it is correctly noted in, for example, 'Diary of Sir Archibald Johnston of Wariston 1639', ed. George M. Paul, in *Miscellany of the Scottish History Society* (Edinburgh 1896), 4-5 and Brown, op. cit., 484

[8] Vaughan T. Wells, 'The Origins of Covenanting Thought and Resistance: *c.* 580-1638' (Ph. D. thesis, Department of History, University of Stirling 1997), 191-192

[9] *Register of the Privy Council of Scotland 1616-1619*, ed. David Masson, (Edinburgh 1894), vol. xi, pp. lxiii-lxiv, 598-600

[10] *The Diary of Sir Archibald Johnston of Wariston 1632-39*, ed. G.M. Paul (Scottish History Society 1911), xii, 7, 10, 12, 13, 179, 182

[11] Ibid., 185

[12] ECA, MS Dean of Guild Accounts 1626-1720, n/p, 1631-2

[13] NRS, Wills and Testaments, Edinburgh Commissary Court, CC8/8/56/384-6 (Sir James Skene); James Brown, *The Epitaphs and Monumental Inscriptions in Greyfriars Churchyard* (Edinburgh 1867), 293

[14] 'Diary of Sir Archibald Johnston of Wariston 1639', ed. G. M. Paul, in *Miscellany of the Scottish History Society* (Edinburgh 1896), 5; *Register of the Great Seal 1634-1651*, no. 666, p.238; NRS, Wills and Testaments, Edinburgh Commissary Court, CC8/8/59/503-507 (James Inglis)

# 30

## *Eleanor Maule, Lady Prestongrange*

Eleanor Maule's forebears had been robust, popular and prolific lairds in Angus, but William Maule, her father, was the youngest of fourteen sons and he had decided to seek his fortune in Edinburgh. There he established a successful business as a merchant and married Bethia Guthrie, the Town Clerk's daughter. In her right, he became a burgess, was elected to the Town Council and some time before 1607 served as Dean of Guild.[1] He and Bethia and their children would have attended St Giles', where he seems to have occupied a prominent role. After John Durie, one of the ministers, delivered a series of sermons criticising royal policies, James VI forbade him to preach and exiled him from Edinburgh. Eleanor's father was one of the Town Council's commissioners sent in 1582 to Perth, in an initially successful attempt to persuade the King to allow Durie to return.[2]

Maule and Bethia had no sons, but Eleanor was the fourth of their seven daughters. We do not know when she and her sisters were born, but she was also the fourth to marry. Her father was still alive, and no doubt arranged the match with Alexander Morrison of Prestongrange, a promising young lawyer who was to bring her a more prominent position in society than any of her sisters would achieve. Their wedding took place in Edinburgh on 6 September 1610.[3] Morrison, born in 1579, would have been some years older than she was. He came from a well-known merchant family and his younger brother Isaac was the wealthy merchant who married Helen Arnot **(11)**. However, their mother was a daughter of the Lord President of the Court of Session, and probably under his influence Eleanor's husband studied law. He became an advocate in 1604 and on 14 February 1626 he was made a Lord of Session with the title of Lord Prestongrange. He took this name from the estate in East Lothian which he had purchased four years earlier as his family's country home[4]. Two years later, he became the second Rector of Edinburgh University.[5]

Details of Eleanor's married life are few. She had various sons and daughters. The eldest son was Alexander, there was a daughter Bethia **(31)**, a second daughter named Catherine and another daughter who married a man named Marjoribanks, but the first names of that daughter and any other children are unknown. Possibly they did not all survive to adult life.[6] Eleanor's father died in 1619 and in 1622 she and several of her sisters were the executors of their mother's Testament.[7] Seven years later, on Saturday 6 June 1629, her daughter Bethia was married at Preston-grange to Sir Robert Spottiswoode.[8] Two years after that, Eleanor was widowed, when her husband died on 20 September 1631 at the age of fifty-one.[9] He had made his Testament at Prestongrange three weeks earlier.

Eleanor took the Testament for registration, 'as having the best knowledge' of his business, and on behalf of their eldest son Alexander, who was still a minor. It shows that she and her husband had enjoyed an impressive lifestyle. He left a library of books estimated to be worth 6000 merks as well as an expensive array of silver, which indicates that they must have entertained in considerable style. There was a vastly expensive great silver basin and ewer, double overgilt [twice gilded], worth no less than £648, a double overgilt salt estimated at £181 and three more double overgilt cups with covers, valued at between £20 and £123 each. There were two great silver mazers [large cups], various small silver single overgilt cups and salts and three dozen silver spoons, one of the sets double overgilt.

Their furnishings were divided between the house at Prestongrange and their Edinburgh home and their goods, together with the debts owed to Eleanor's husband, were worth an astonishing £58,219. However, his own debts exceeded his goods and the money owed to him by over £30,000. This did not mean that he was in financial trouble. On the contrary, it was a sign that he was very active in both his legal career and in money-lending. He does not refer to Eleanor by name in his Will, but she features as his 'dear wife' and she and various friends, including Lewis Stewart and Thomas Hope, were to help to look after the interests of his 'remnant' children, the term possibly indicating that some of his offspring had died. He added that his eldest son Alexander was to make sure that the provisions he had made for Eleanor and the younger children were paid.[10]

At some point in 1631-2, probably before her husband's death, a seat was put up for Eleanor in St Giles' and it is mentioned again in 1633-34. Her daughter Lady Spottiswoode's seat was also erected in 1631-2, both probably in expectation of Charles I's intended visit.[11] Eleanor did not marry again. She would have had a liferent of the house at Prestongrange, and it is noted in the mid-1630s that she owned but rented out a house on the south side of the High Street, near the Canongate. She lived in a much smaller house in the same area, probably having moved to it when she was widowed.[12]

Eleanor made her Will on 28 October 1663. Her sole executor was to be her son Sir Alexander Morrison, 'out of my love and affection to him', and to her two grandchildren, Eleanor and Marion Marjoribanks, she left her clothing. The former was also to have the linen in 'my rich coffer.' She died just over a year later, in November 1664. At that time she had one servant, Jean Boyd, but her possessions were few: some old furnishings in her chamber estimated at only 50 merks and a house clock worth £18. Her son owed her an annuity of 400 merks for that year, and she herself left a few debts, including £40 due to James Borthwick and Mark Hamilton, apothecaries, for drugs and medicaments supplied by them during her illness. In all, when the £106 she owed was deducted, she left only £349:10/-.[13]

---

[1] *Scots Peerage*, vii, 10-14; *Register of the Great Seal of Scotland A.D.1593-1608*, ed. John Maitland Thomson (Edinburgh 1890), 712 no. 1961; 723 no. 1990; NRS, Wills and Testaments, Edinburgh Commissary Court, CC8/8/50/636 (William Maule); ibid., CC8/8/54/346 (Bethia Guthrie)

[2] *Edinburgh Burgh Extracts 1573-1589*, 568; J. Cameron Lees, *St Giles', Edinburgh: Church, College and Cathedral* (Edinburgh 1889), 277

[3] *Scots Peerage*, vii, 14; *The Register of Marriages for the Parish of Edinburgh 1595-1700*, ed. Henry Paton (Scottish Record Society 1905), 459

[4] *Scots Peerage*, v, 469

[5] Brunton, *Lords of Session*, 275

[6] NRS, Wills and Testaments, Edinburgh Commissary Court, CC8/8/71/860, 862 (Hellenor Maule) and CC8/8/55/452 (Alexander Morrison, Lord Prestongrange); D. Stevenson, 'Spottiswood, Sir Robert, Lord Dunipace, *ODNB* (Oxford University Press 2004); Diary of Sir Archibald Johnston of Wariston 1632-1639, ed. George Morison Paul (Scottish History Society 1911), p. xxi

[7] NRS, Wills and Testaments, Edinburgh Commissary Court, CC8/8/50/636 (William Maule) and CC8/8/54/346-47 (Bethia Guthrie)

[8] NLS, Alexander Spotswood papers, MS48.02, copy letter of Robert Spottiswoode to his children, 1646

[9] Brunton, *Lords of Session*, 251

[10] NRS, Wills and Testaments, Edinburgh Commissary Court, CC8/8/55/449-53 (Alexander Morrison, Lord Prestongrange)

[11] ECA, MS Dean of Guild Accounts 1626-1720, 1631-32 pp.9, 15

[12] *Edinburgh Housemails Taxation Book*, 226-227

[13] NRS, Wills and Testaments, Edinburgh Commissary Court, CC8/8/71/860-862 (Hellenor Maule)

# 31

## *Bethia Morrison, Lady Sweetheart*

At the same time that Lady Prestongrange **(30)** had her seat put up in St Giles' in 1631-32, so too did her daughter gain a seat of her own. Six pounds was the sum spent on Bethia Morrison's, who was known at the time as 'Lord Sweetheart's Lady', the term accorded to her in the Dean of Guild's accounts.[1] This beguiling title had no immediate romantic connotations, however. On Saturday, 6 June 1629, Bethia had been married at her parent's home to Sir Robert Spottiswoode.[2] A Lord of Session aged thirty-three, he was the son of the Protestant Archbishop of St Andrews, John Spottiswoode, and through his father's influence he had obtained the former lands of Sweetheart Abbey in Dumfries. It was by then officially known as New Abbey and, for obvious reasons, when Spottiswoode became a judge, he chose as his title 'Lord New Abbey' although 'Lord Sweetheart' obviously remained current in local circles.[3]

Spottiswoode's career was advancing rapidly by then and four years after his marriage to Bethia he became Lord President of the Court of Session, nominated by Charles I himself. His support for the King's ecclesiastical policies and the fact that he was the son of an archbishop made him increasingly unpopular, however.[4] He and Bethia shared with his father a very large house, probably in the Cowgate, just to the west of St Giles'.[5] According to a list made by her husband, Bethia gave birth to their first child, a son, in Edinburgh on 22 February 1630. They named him John, after her husband's father the Archbishop, and he was baptised in St Giles' on 6 March by John Maxwell, minister of the Auld Kirk.[6]

In the summer of 1631 Bethia went home to Prestongrange to see her father, who was seriously ill. She was heavily pregnant at the time, and her second son was born there at 3 a.m. on 26 August. Two days later the baby was baptised Alexander, in the local church. He was called after her sick father, who died three and a half weeks after that. Bethia's five subsequent children were all born in Edinburgh, their arrival carefully recorded by their father. Eleanor, called after Bethia's mother, came along on 26 March 1633 and was baptised by John Maxwell just before he became Bishop of Ross, but she died the following January. William, born in December 1634, was baptised by Andrew Ramsay, by then minister of the Auld Kirk.[7] That baby died in infancy but was followed by Rachel, on 21 March 1636, named after Spottiswoode's mother and also baptised by Ramsay. Robert was born on 17 September 1637 and baptised by James Hannay, the Dean of St Giles', who had recently had a prayer book hurled at his head, reputedly by Jenny Geddes, when he attempted to read from it for the first time.[8] Had Bethia and her husband been at that service? Perhaps. According to Spottiswoode, the new baby was not named after himself but for his friend the young Robert, 8th Lord Boyd, who was the infant's chief godfather.

Finally, on the morning of 22 October 1639, Bethia gave birth to a daughter, who was baptised that same evening by Andrew Ramsay. The swift baptism indicates that the baby was considered to be unlikely to survive. Indeed, little Bethia lived for only three months, and it seems likely that her mother had died giving birth to her. Spottiswoode wrote a sorrowful Latin epitaph for his wife, dated 1639, praising her piety and her prudence, and adding that favourite seventeenth-century compliment: 'She had a mind more masculine than feminine.'[9] He did not remarry, and seven years later he would be executed for having been in the royalist army of the Marquis of Montrose at the Battle of Philiphaugh. It was his last letter to his children which recorded for them that list with the times of their births, and urged them never to oppose their monarch, for any cause whatsoever.[10]

---

[1]ECA, MS Dean of Guild Accounts, 1626-1720, 1631-32, n/p

[2] NLS, Alexander Spotswood [sic] Papers, MS 48.02 Copy list of Sir Robert Spottiswoode entitled 'The day of my Children's birth', 1646

[3] Stevenson, David, 'Spottiswood [Spottiswoode], Sir Robert, Lord Dunipace', ODNB (Oxford University Press 2004); A.S. Wayne Pearce, 'John Spottiswoode, Archbishop of St Andrews and historian', in ibid.

[4] Stevenson, op. cit.

[5] Edinburgh Housemails Taxation Book, 515

[6] NLS, MS 48.02 (as above); James Cameron Lees, St Giles' Edinburgh, Church, College and Cathedral, (Edinburgh 1889), 280

[7]NLS, MS 48.02; Lees, op. cit., 280-281

[8] NLS, MS 48.02; Lees, op. cit., 288

[9] NLS, MS 48.02, copy epitaph by Sir Robert Spottiswoode, 1639. I am grateful to Roy Pinkerton for his advice on the Latin epitaph and its English translation

[10] Edward J. Cowan, Montrose: For Covenant and King (London 1977), 241-242; NLS, MS 48.02, op. cit.

# 32

## *Margaret Winram, Mrs Stewart*

During the year 1631-32, a seat was made and put up in St Giles' for Lewis Stewart's wife[1]. Her name was Margaret Winram, but it has always been said that her parentage is unknown. In part, this is probably because the task of researchers has been complicated by the fact that Winrams feature in the records in a tantalising variety of spellings including Windrahame, Wynrahame and even Vinerame. There was no knowing whether any of the people thus indexed in lists of burgesses, apprentices and so forth could have been Margaret's father. In the end, however, careful scrutiny of the Will of a very wealthy lawyer, James Winram of Liberton, provides the answer.[2]

By his own account, James Winram lived to a great age, and when he finally died in April 1632 he left over £20,000. Not only had he built a burial aisle for himself at Liberton Church, but in 1617 he had purchased Inch House, a fifteenth-century tower house. Now a community centre and part of Edinburgh, is still bears the carved initials of himself and his wife, Jean Swinton.[3] Moreover his Testament not only lists his goods but copies his Will, signed on 17 March 1632. In it he makes a special bequest to the six children of Lewis Stewart and his wife Margaret, whom Winram specifies as being his own daughter. It also mentions Margaret's only daughter, Jean.

It was on 1 September 1613 that Margaret had married the young advocate, Lewis Stewart, who would make a name for himself not only for his astute mind and his erudition but by assembling an important collection of historical manuscripts now preserved in the National Library of Scotland.[4] By the mid-1630s he had acquired five properties in the vicinity of St Giles', including various shops and a tavern, which he rented out.[5] His career is well known, but we have only a tantalising glimpse of Margaret, whose own claim to fame is that she was for a short time the mother-in-law of Archibald Johnston of Warriston, the famous co-author of the National Covenant.

In 1632 when he was twenty, Johnston had become increasingly worried. He was attracted physically to several women but he was anxious not to give way to these sexual feelings outside matrimony. He therefore decided that he must find a wife. He was a member of a strict religious family, and in fact he was living in Sciennes in the household of the formidable Covenanting Rachel Arnot at the time. He was very nervous about choosing someone whom God did not intend him to marry. His father was dead, so to seek advice he went first of all across to Durie in Fife. His aunt, Margaret Craig (23) was married to Lord Durie the judge and he wanted to hear his opinion. Durie told him to ignore his own preferences and the urging of friends and instead simply concentrate on choosing a young woman who would be acceptable to God.[6]

This apparently did not apply to those Warriston had in mind, so on his return to Edinburgh he accompanied another uncle to the Communion service at Liberton, hoping to take a look at various possible candidates. Someone had mentioned Jean Stewart, Margaret's daughter, but he had been told that she was very young and could not be married until another year had passed. Moreover, not only had her complexion had been ruined by smallpox, but her father was likely to consider Warriston to be too poor to provide for her. Reluctantly, he asked someone to point her out, but he then mistook 'Maggie Windram' for her daughter Jean Stewart. This seems odd, for Margaret must have been at least in her mid-thirties by then. However, muffled up against the winter cold in the elaborate costume of the time and presumably seated at some distance away from Johnston, next to her daughter, his error was perhaps understandable.

Most of the Johnston family were by now enthusiastic about Jean, and approached her father, who responded favourably. Warriston was still a reluctant suitor, for his aunt, Lady Curriehill **(29)**, was now insisting that Jean was too young, probably not yet fourteen. Nevertheless, upon reflection, he decided that her youth was no disadvantage as he would see to it that, under his tutelage, she would grow up to be as pious as he was himself. They were married on 23 October 1632 at 7 o'clock (morning or evening unspecified) in the Auld Kirk of St Giles'. Their marriage was a success, but Jean died on 12 June 1633. The cause of her death is said to be unknown, but in his diary her devastated husband mentioned that two nights earlier 'she took her crying'. This seems vague enough, but at that period it had a specific meaning. Nowadays we would say 'her labour started', so she died in childbirth.

Trying to console him, Jean Winram, Margaret's Winram's sister, told Johnston 'some good things and signs of grace' in Margaret herself, which made him thank God that his mother-in-law had been 'of the seed of the faithful'.[7] By this time, however, Margaret herself had died. Although she had been in Liberton Church that day in early 1632, she was dead by the time her father wrote his Will on 17 March that year, when he referred to her as 'his late daughter, Margaret'.

[1] ECA, MS Dean of Guild Accounts 1626-1720, 1631-32, n/p

[2] NRS, Wills and Testaments, Edinburgh Commissary Court, CC8/8/55/644-650 (James Winram)

[3] Inch House Community Centre, http://canmore.org.uk/site/52547

[4] *Register of Marriages for the Parish of Edinburgh 1595-1700* ed. Henry Paton (Scottish Record Society 1905), 752; Theo Van Heijnsbergen, 'Literature and History in Queen Mary's Edinburgh' in *The Renaissance in Scotland: Studies in Literature, Religion, History and Culture* eds A. A. MacDonald, Michael Lynch, Ian Cowan (Brill, 1994), 220; NLS, The Historical Collections of Sir Lewis Stewart, NLS, Adv. MS22.1.14

[5] *Edinburgh Housemails Taxation Book*, 173, 205, 219, 343

[6] *Diary of Sir Archibald Johnston of Wariston 1632-1639* ed. George Morison Paul (Scottish History Society 1911), 1-4

[7] Ibid., 5, 6-8, 10, 12-13, 62

# 33

## *Marion Nicoll, Mrs Aikenhead*

Marion Nicoll's parentage is not recorded, although there were quite a few Nicoll merchants and craftsmen in Edinburgh who could have been her relatives. Her date of birth has not been found either, but what we do know is that in 1631-2, as the wife of David Aikenhead, she had a seat put up for her in St Giles' at a cost of £9:17:4. The Dean of Guild paid a further £13 when it was mended in 1634-35, so it must have been fairly impressive.[1] This was not surprising, for her husband was a well-known merchant burgess of Edinburgh.[2] Over the years he served as a bailie of the town, was Dean of Guild for seven years, and indeed was Lord Provost three times, in 1620-22, 1625-29 and from 1634 until his death in 1637.[3]

Marion and he lived in part of what is now Fleshmarket Close, then known as Provost's Close because his house was there.[4] In 1617 they jointly acquired the lands of Kilquhis Wester in the Presbytery of Cupar, in Fife.[5] Given the difficulties of early seventeenth-century travel this is rather surprising, but perhaps there may have been some family connection to one or the other of them. They had three sons, Henry, Alexander and David, and St Giles' must have loomed large in their lives.[6] They would have been members of the congregation, with Aikenhead sitting in the Town Council Loft and eventually in his special seat there as Lord Provost.

Moreover, while he was Dean of Guild from 1613-20 he was very much involved in the endless repairs to the roof and gutters of the church. By 1615 he was busy repairing the Town Council's loft inside the East Kirk, the following year he was told to open up again the two windows in that part, which had previously been blocked up with stone and lime, presumably at the time of the Reformation, and then he had to make sure that glass was put in them once more. Also in 1616, he was instructed by the Town Council to make a loft in the East Kirk for the bishops, in keeping with James VI's ecclesiastical policies.[7]

When Marion's three sons grew up, both Henry and Alexander became burgesses of Edinburgh in 1631 and 1630 respectively. Henry was a graduate and Alexander found a career as a Writer to the Signet, but David's occupation is not known. Aikenhead himself died on 13 August 1637 nominating 'his loving wife' Marion and their sons as his executors. He was not as wealthy as might have been expected, although he left 1300 merks in ready money, 'lying beside him'. His utensils, furnishings and silverwork were valued at a further 1000 merks and once his debts in and out were included, his free gear amounted to almost £1500 pounds. He had probably spent so much time on his official business for the town that his original merchant activities had suffered. His Will, written on 2 January that same year, included charitable bequests to the Edinburgh Hospital, 'the prisoners' and to the town' burgesses.

He also explained that he was anxious to avoid the kind of arguments that often arose among a man's children when he had died. 'I leave my wife and my children my blessing', he said, 'praying my wife to continue [to be] a loving mother to her children and mine' and urging the children to be 'loving, comfortable and obedient' to their mother. They must fear God, love one another and live as honest men so that they were profitable members of God's

Kirk, their country and commonwealth. He relied upon his cousin, the Lord Clerk Register John Hay, to make sure that his wishes were carried out, asking that when the end came he should be laid in the earth with the rest of the faithful.

The town council had some time before granted him the unusual honour of being buried inside Greyfriars Church. Only a select few were buried inside churches in the aftermath of the Reformation, for the Reformers disapproved of this mark of distinction.[8] However, he must indeed have been buried inside Greyfriars, for his memorial, noting that he was 71 when he died, was built into the north wall of the interior and was only removed from inside the church in 1845 after a fire there.[9] Marion duly registered his Testament on 14 September 1637. Her own date of death is unknown.

---

[1] ECA, MS Dean of Guild Accounts, 1626-1720, 1631-32 n/p

[2] NRS, Menzies of Menzies Papers, GD1/501/50, 56, Discharges by Aikenhead to Sir Alexander Menzies of that ilk

[3] *The Lord Provosts of Edinburgh*, 36; William Maitland, *The History of Edinburgh from its foundation to the present time* (Edinburgh 1753), 227

[4] Canmore website: http://canmore.org.uk/collection/460294; *Edinburgh Housemails Taxation Book*, 187

[5] *The Register of the Great Seal of Scotland 1609-1620*, ed. John Maitland Thomson (Edinburgh 1892), 597-98, no. 1651

[6] NRS, Wills and Testaments, Edinburgh Commissary Court, CC8/8/58/387 (David Aikenhead)

[7] *Edinburgh Burgh Extracts 1604-1625*, 116, 123, 131, 135, 141, 152

[8] NRS, CC8/8/58/385-389 (David Aikenhead)

[9] James Brown, *The Most Famous Epitaphs and Monumental Inscriptions in the Greyfriars Churchyard, Edinburgh* (Edinburgh 1901), 294, 296; http://www.gravestonephotos.com accessed 10 July 2018

# 34

## *Marion Scott, Lady Hatton*

Marion Scott was granted her own seat in St Giles' in 1631-32.[1] She was the daughter of the leading lawyer, Laurence Scott of Harperrig and Clerkington, one of the Principal Clerks of Session and Clerk to the Privy Council, and his wife Elizabeth Pringle. Originally from an Ayrshire family, he had become an advocate in Edinburgh in 1607 and soon began to accumulate extensive properties in Midlothian, beginning with Harperrig, about twelve miles south-west of Edinburgh and then adding other estates in the Ratho area.[2] Marion was his eldest daughter and by 1617 she was married to Mr James Scott, a brother of Sir John Scot of Scotstarvet, Director of the Chancery. They were from a Perthshire branch of the Scott family and although the surname of Sir John, author of *The Staggering State of Scottish Statesmen*, is invariably given as 'Scot', Marion's husband always features in the records as 'Scott'.[3]

She and he had two daughters, Elspeth and Jean.[4] In 1617 their family life was disturbed by a startling incident. The goods of a man named Gavin Scott, probably a relative, had been forfeited, either because he had been convicted of a criminal offence or more likely because he had died intestate. At any rate, both Marion's husband and an Edinburgh burgess named James Harper had laid claim to his goods. These were awarded to Harper, but before he could arrange to take possession of them, Marion's husband and her father turned up in 'warlike attire' with five or six armed companions at the house where the dead man's goods were being stored. Harper was there already and a fierce quarrel ensued, the Scotts apparently striking him with knives and carrying off the goods themselves. As a result, they were summoned before the Privy Council and sentenced to be committed to Edinburgh Castle, at their own expense.[5]

Precisely when Marion's father was Clerk to the Privy Council is unclear but, with his connections, he and her husband were probably released soon afterwards. Her father's reputation was certainly untarnished, for in the following year he received from Charles I the lands of Bavelaw, followed by those of Bonnington in 1629.[6] Not long after that, Marion's husband died, but in about 1630 she married again. Her second husband was her father's immediate neighbour, Richard Lauder, the 11th and last Laird of Hatton, which adjoined Bonnington. He was the stepson of Annabella Bellenden (17). More active locally than on a national scale, Lauder had sat briefly in the Scottish Parliament of 1621 and, during his marriage to Marion, he was on the committee of war for Edinburgh during 1647 and 1648. Eventually in 1663 he became a Justice of the Peace. Marion and he had three daughters, Joanna, Jean and Elizabeth.[7]

The family would have divided their time between his main properties. His medieval tower house at Hatton was set in pleasant parkland and, in his grandfather's day, James VI had liked to visit for the sake of the excellent hunting there.[8] Hatton also rented a house in Edinburgh, just west of St Giles', and he had acquired additional lands in East Lothian and the Borders.[9] When Marion's father died in 1637, he was unusually careful in making bequests to his various granddaughters. He bequeathed the sum of 1000 merks each to Marion's two daughters, Elspeth and

Jean, by her first husband, James Scott. He also left 1000 merks to Marion herself, along with her husband Richard Lauder and their daughters.[10]

Jean Lauder would marry Sir John Erskine of Calderhall in 1650, and two years later her younger sister Elizabeth became the wife of Charles Maitland, the future 3rd Earl of Lauderdale, with the marriage feast being held at Hatton. This was an important alliance. Since Elizabeth's father had no male heirs, it had been agreed as part of the marriage negotiations that the liferent of Hatton would be settled on the bride and groom. Maitland was to take the surname of Lauder, his coat of arms would be quartered with Elizabeth's, and the Hatton estate would become part of the Lauderdale properties once her father was dead.[11]

Marion died in July 1665, when John Lamont recorded in his diary the sudden death of 'old Lady Hatton'. She was buried at Ratho Parish Church, where the Lauders had their family vault.[12] Her husband lived on for another ten years, dying 'in the Abbey of Holyroodhouse' at the age of 86. His body was taken home to the House of Hatton and he was buried at Ratho Parish Church on 29 November 1675.[13]

---

[1] ECA, MS Dean of Guild Accounts 1626-1720; 1631-2, n/p

[2] John Alexander Inglis, *The Monros of Auchinbowie* (Edinburgh 1911), 170-80; John Burke, *A Genealogical and Heraldic History of the Commoners of Great Britain and Ireland* (London 1836), 171-72; NRS, Papers of the Dick-Lauder Family of Fountainhall, GD41/287, Extract Procuratory of Resignation to Elizabeth Pringle, widow of Laurence Scott of Clerkington, advocate; Colin McWilliam and Christopher Wilson, *Lothian, except Edinburgh (London 1980)*, 98

[3] Stevenson, D., 'Scot of Scotstarvit, *ODNB* (Oxford University Press 2004)

[4] NRAS, Wills and Testaments, Edinburgh Commissary Court, CC8/8/71/498-502 (Laurence Scott)

[5] *The Register of the Privy Council of Scotland AD 1616-1619*, (Edinburgh 1894), ed. David Masson 263-264; Inglis, op. cit., 180-181

[6] K.M. Brown et al eds (St Andrews 2007-18) *The Records of the Parliament of Scotland to 1707*, ratified 17 November 1641, NAS, PA2/22, f. 275v-275v; *The Register of the Great Seal of Scotland AD 1620-1633* ed. John Maitland Thomson (Edinburgh 1894), 465, no. 1374; Colin McWilliam and Christopher Wilson, *Lothian, except Edinburgh*, (London 1980), 98

[7] *Notes and Historical References to the Lauder Family*, ed. James Young, (Glasgow 1884), lvi, 72-3; *The Register of the Great Seal of Scotland AD 1660-1668*, ed. John Horne Stevenson (Edinburgh 1914), no. 295, pp.149-50

[8] Canmore website: https://canmore.org.uk/site/50361/hatton-house

[9] *Edinburgh Housemails Taxation Book*, 509

[10] NRAS, Wills and Testaments, Edinburgh Commissary Court, CC8/8/71/498-502 (Laurence Scott)

[11] *The Register of the Great Seal of Scotland AD 1660-1668*, no. 26, pp.8-11

[12] Lamont, *Diary*, 180; http://canmore.org.uk/site/50361

[13] *Index to genealogies, birthbriefs and funeral escutcheons recorded in the Lyon Office*, ed. Francis Grant (Scottish Record Society 1908), 32

# 35

## *Elizabeth Morrison, Lady Dick*

Elizabeth Morrison came from a well-known Edinburgh merchant family. Her father, John Morrison, was a prominent burgess of the town.[1] Her mother, Katherine Preston, probably had a similar background, since Prestons who were merchants and lawyers feature in the Edinburgh testaments and marriage records.[2] Known to her five siblings as Bessie, Elizabeth was the youngest daughter.[3] Her eldest brother became the judge, Lord Prestongrange, and was married to Eleanor Maule **(30)**, the second eldest was Isaac Morrison, husband of Helen Arnot **(11)**, while Bethia Morrison **(31)** who became the wife of Sir Robert Spottiswoode in 1629 was her niece, so Elizabeth was very much a member of the elite society of lawyers and merchants who played such a leading role in Edinburgh life. Moreover, it was Elizabeth who made the best marriage of all when she was married to William Dick, the wealthiest man in Scotland.

Their wedding took place on 15 June 1603[4] and they went on to have at least nine children: John, Margaret, Elizabeth, Katherine **(36)**, Andrew, Alexander, Lewis, William and Christian.[5] By 1634-35 Elizabeth Morrison had her own seat in St Giles', for it was being mended that year.[6] It had probably been granted to her two or three years earlier, at a time when her husband was enjoying great prosperity. In addition to his lucrative trade with the Baltic and the Mediterranean, he had invested in coal, salt and the manufacture of soap. He had also engaged in money lending not only to fellow merchants but to landowners and indeed to James VI himself, and subsequently to Charles I, thereby gaining royal favour.

On 2 August 1631 Dick and Elizabeth purchased the Edinburgh estate of Braid, including Greenbank and Plewlands, on condition that she gave up her entitlement to the lands of St Giles' Grange which her husband had very recently acquired.[7] The acquisition of Braid brought with it Craighouse, a handsome sixteenth-century mansion which overlooked the town and exists to this day. The Dick family already occupied a large house and yard near St Giles', stretching back towards the Nor' Loch, as well as several other houses and a shop, which he now rented out.[8] In 1638 Dick was appointed Lord Provost of Edinburgh,[9] in 1641 he received a knighthood,[10] presumably as a reward for his loans to Charles I, but although he is not mentioned as playing any part in the so-called Jenny Geddes riot of 1637 he was, in fact, deeply opposed to the King's ecclesiastical policies as were many of the other merchants.

In 1646 Charles made him a baronet of Nova Scotia, perhaps in the vain hope of detaching him from the Covenanting side, but disaster followed.[11] The vast sums of money he had lent to the Covenanters were never repaid, leaving him ruined. He led the deputation which welcomed Cromwell to Edinburgh in 1652, but he left soon afterwards for London. Taking lodgings in Westminster, he issued numerous petitions pleading for reimbursement. Whether Elizabeth really accompanied him is unclear, but all his efforts failed, and he died there on 19 December 1655. Her date of death is unknown.[12]

His dramatic descent from wealth and favour impressed not only contemporaries but future generations, who saw it as epitomising the transitory nature of worldly success.

Two years after his death *The lamentable estate and distressed case of the deceased Sir William Dick in Scotland and his numerous family and creditors* was published in London, and subsequently a legend grew up to the effect that he had been thrown into prison, where he died.[13] In the late 18th century an engraving showing three views of him was reproduced many times. On the left, entitled 'Prosperity', he stands happily in fashionable clothing. In the centre, 'In Prison', he sits, downcast, his wrists chained together, while to the right, 'Death' depicts him lying in his coffin.[14]

Equally popular was a poignant oil painting of the same era, which would be engraved many times. It purports to show him sitting in prison with a couple of guards behind him. Beside him stands a youthful Elizabeth, clad all in white, with a white veil over her head and her hands clasped together as she looks sadly down at him. Three of their small children gaze sorrowfully at him too, adding to the pathos of the scene. In reality, they had long been adults in 1655, their father was in his mid-seventies by then, and if Elizabeth was still alive, she would have been married for 52 years.[15] Despite her husband's death in London, he and she would both be buried in Greyfriars Churchyard, with most of their children.[16]

[1] Stewart, L., 'Dick, Sir William, of Braid', *ODNB* (Oxford University Press 2004)

[2] e.g. *The Register of Marriages for the Parish of Edinburgh (1595-1700)* ed. Henry Paton (Scottish Record Society 1905), 553; *Register of Edinburgh Testaments* i, 16, 223; ii, 324

[3] NRS, Wills and Testaments, Edinburgh Commissary Court, CC8/8/54/155 (Helen Morrison)

[4] *The Register of Marriages for the Parish of Edinburgh (1595-1700)*, 491

[5] *Antiquity of the Family of Dick, extracted from Playfair's British Antiquity* (London 1826), 12-13; Stewart, L., 'Dick, Sir William, of Braid', *ODNB* (Oxford University Press 2004)

[6] ECA, MS Dean of Guild Accounts, 1626-1720, 1634-35, n/p

[7] *The Register of the Great Seal of Scotland A.D. 1620-1633*, ed. J. Maitland Thomson (Edinburgh 1894), no. 1834, pp.629-30

[8] *Edinburgh Housemails Taxation Book*, 102, 125, 134, 141, 387, 100, 126

[9] *Lord Provosts of Edinburgh*, 40-41

[10] *Antiquity of the Family of Dick*, 10; *The Register of the Privy Council of Scotland AD 1638-1643*, second series, vii (Edinburgh 1906), 142

[11] John Burke, *A General and Heraldic Dictionary of the Peerage and Baronetage of the British Empire*, i, (London 1832), 361

[12] Stewart, '*Dick, Sir William, of Braid*', *ODNB* (Oxford University Press 2004)

[13] Thomas Finlay Henderson, 'William Dick', in *Dictionary of National Biography* (original publication 1885-1900), xv, 19-20

[14] National Portrait Gallery, London, NPGD 27246, attributed to an artist of the circle of William Hamilton

[15] *Sir William Dick in Prison 1655*, attributed to an artist of the circle of William Hamilton, sold at Christies Amsterdam, 2011

[16] James Brown, *The Epitaphs and Monumental Inscriptions in Greyfriars Churchyard* (Edinburgh 1867), lxvii

# 36

## Katherine Dick, Lady Nisbet

The list of people who received seats of their own in St Giles' in 1631-32 is slightly puzzling. Sir William Nisbet and Lady Hatton **(34)** are named consecutively, and then Nisbet's wife is mentioned, her seat costing £3:10/-.[1] There is nothing surprising about the separation of the names of husband and wife, however. Their seats would have been made at slightly different times. What is odd is that Nisbet's wife, Katherine Dick, had died in 1630.[2] He did not remarry, his son William, still a minor, did not find a wife until 1642[3] and there were no other relevant Nisbets in the area. The most likely explanation is that Lady Nisbet's seat was commissioned shortly before she died, but was not paid for by the Dean of Guild until eight or nine months later and so did not feature in his accounts until then.

Nisbet had probably known Katherine all her life[4], for her father, Sir William Dick of Braid, was a close friend of his. Both men were highly prosperous Edinburgh merchants engaged in lucrative foreign trade, both would serve as Lord Provost more than once, and Dick was undisputedly the richest man in Scotland. Katherine's mother, Elizabeth Morrison **(35)**, came from another well-known Edinburgh merchant family.[5] We do not know Katherine's age at the time of her wedding, but theirs was not a union of two young people, for her bridegroom was eleven years older than her father. In May 1622 Nisbet's first wife, Janet Williamson, had died after more than thirty years of marriage, apparently leaving no surviving children.[6] If he wanted a son to succeed him, he would have to find another wife. Katherine was young and healthy, their marriage contract would no doubt make strict provision for her future when she was widowed, and she would have brought with her a handsome tocher. The wedding seems to have taken place soon after Janet's death and Katherine and her husband settled down in Dean House, then just to the west of Edinburgh.

Nisbet had bought the property in 1609. It was a tower house and he is sometimes credited with having built it, but it seems more likely that he had considerably extended the existing structure. He added to its already extensive grounds, which included several mills, by a further purchase of lands. After completing his second term of office as Lord Provost in 1621, he was not re-elected, having apparently enraged James VI by refusing to support the Five Articles of Perth.[7] Nisbet therefore decided to concentrate on farming his estate at the Dean and lived there permanently, renting out his other large houses in Edinburgh.[8] By his son's time, the Dean lands had extensive crops of barley, oats, wheat and peas growing on them.[9]

Although the house itself was eventually demolished in 1845 to make way for the Dean Cemetery, various carved stones from it have survived, some featuring the initials of Nisbet and his first wife, but others displaying his initials beside those of Katherine. Built into the Dean Cemetery wall, for instance, is a stone with their impaled coats of arms, their initials and, in Latin, the words 'Here my honour was born'. Two other stones with their coats of arms and initials were found at Coltbridge and in Dalry Cemetery.[10] Katherine and her husband had three children, William, Janet and Elizabeth.[11] As we have seen before, husbands sometimes named a second wife's child after their first wife and this would probably explain the choice of their elder daughter's name.[12]

We know something of the interior appearance of Dean House in their time. In keeping with the fashion of the day, the principal room was the handsome Great Hall, which featured a rather unexpected series of pictures set into the ceiling. These depicted religious scenes, including Judith slaying Holofernes and King David playing his harp. (Plate 7) They are believed to have been copies of paintings which decorated the main chamber of the house in Blythe's Close built for the Roman Catholic Mary of Guise in the 1550s when she was Queen Regent of Scotland. The Dean House copies are said to have been painted between 1607 and 1627. If so, then they must have been very familiar to Katherine and her young children, despite the Reformed backgrounds of her husband and herself. Possibly the subjects were acceptable because they did not include any overtly Catholic symbolism but could have been regarded merely as historical scenes from the Bible.[13]

Far from outliving her much older husband, Katherine would sadly die on 13 May 1630. Her younger daughter was only three, the other two children under the age of eight.[14] Sir William Nisbet did not marry again and his life ended nine years later.[15]

---

[1]ECA, MS Dean of Guild Accounts 1626-1720, n/p

[2] NRS, Wills and Testaments, Edinburgh Commissary Court, CC8/8/55/268 (Katherine Dick)

[3] NLS, Acc.10928, photocopy of marriage contract between Sir William Nisbet of Dean and Margaret Murray, 1642, the original in Stirling Council Archives

[4] *Antiquity of the Family of Dick, extracted from Playfair's British Antiquity* (London 1826), 13; *Alexander Nisbet's Heraldic Plates*, v, (Edinburgh 1892), 7

[5] Stewart, L. (2009, October 08). 'Dick, Sir William, of Braid', *ODNB* (Oxford University Press 2004)

[6] NRS, Wills and Testaments, Edinburgh Commissary Court CC8/8/52/403-405 (Janet Williamson)

[7] Laura A.M. Stewart, 'The Political Repercussions of the Five Articles of Perth: A Reassessment of James VI and I's Religious Policies in Scotland' in *The Sixteenth Century Journal*, vol.38, no. 4, (Winter 2007), 1029, where a printing error says that Nisbet demitted office in 1619 instead of 1621

[8] *Edinburgh Housemails Taxation Book*, 183

[9] John Geddie, 'Sculptured Stones of Old Edinburgh: The Dean Group' in *Book of the Old Edinburgh Club*, i (Edinburgh 1908), 97-99; NRS, Wills and Testaments, Edinburgh Commissary Court, CC8/8/68/493-4 (Sir William Nisbet)

[10] Geddie, op. cit., 102-105; description: Canmore website: https://canmore.org.uk/collection/533206; Description with photographs of the stones: http://www.stravaiging.com/history/castle/dean-house

[11] NRS, Wills and Testaments, Edinburgh Commissary Court, CC8/8/55/268 (Katherine Dick)

[12] For example, Margaret Hay, Countess of Dunfermline **(15)**

[13] http://www.stravaiging.com/history/castle/dean-house; National Museum of Scotland, Dean House copies of Mary of Guise paintings, H.KL.68 to H.KL.72. See Plate 7

[14] NRS, Wills and Testaments, Edinburgh Commissary Court, CC8/8/55/268 (Katherine Dick)

[15] Geddie, op. cit., 9

# 37

## *Marjorie Graeme, Lady Newton*

Marjorie Graeme was the daughter of Patrick Graeme, 3rd Laird of Inchbrackie and his first wife Nichola Browne. She was brought up in their tower house at Inchbrackie, near Crieff in Perthshire and on 28 December 1607 she married James Oliphant of Muirhouse, bringing with her a handsome tocher of 7000 merks.[1] He too came from a Perthshire family, but his father, Sir William Oliphant of Newton, was based in Edinburgh, where he was a distinguished lawyer and would become Lord Advocate in 1612.[2] Marjorie's husband had followed his father into the law. He became an advocate, and after his father's death in 1628 he inherited Sir William's estate of Muirhouse, near Cramond. Marjorie and he probably lived there for much of the time, for there is no record of him having owned or rented a house in Edinburgh in the mid-1630s.[3] It was in 1631-32 that her seat in St Giles' was made for her.[4]

Marjorie had at least five children: James, William, George, Nichola (called after her maternal grandmother) and Margaret.[5] Most of them would have been teenagers at the time of an unpleasant incident involving their father in December 1627, when Oliphant reportedly shot dead his gardener. He protested that it had simply been an accident, adding that in any case the victim was not his own gardener. Walking on his lands of Muirhouse with two companions, he had come upon a trespasser who turned out to be a man named William Hair, formerly a gardener at Dean House. Oliphant claimed that, acting in his role as a Justice of the Peace, he challenged the man. Hair at once threatened him with a long-barrelled gun which he was carrying, whereupon Oliphant promptly shot him dead. He and his companions were charged with murder as a result, but on 15 January 1628 they were granted a remission on the grounds that Hair's death had been accidental. According to his contemporary, Scot of Scotstarvet, Oliphant was forced to resign as a Lord of Session as a result.[6] That cannot have been true, however, for he was not appointed to that position until 3 November 1629, and was knighted not long afterwards.[7]

Marjorie's relationship with her husband may well have been difficult. In about 1641 she was living in the family home at Newton of Condie in Perthshire with her eldest son, James. Her husband was presumably in Edinburgh. That seems to have been a fairly permanent arrangement until she suffered a tragic end. Returning home drunk one evening, her son discovered his mother engaged in an adulterous relationship with the local minister. Drawing his sword, James stabbed her to death and would have killed the minister too, but 'the clerical paramour' escaped by leaping over an exceptionally high gate which was thereafter known to the local people as 'the Parson's Gate'. James fled to Ireland, and in his absence, he was sentenced to death for matricide. The lawyers argued that because he and his mother had been living together, she was therefore under his protection and so 'in trust', violation of which meant that he had committed treason as well as murder. Her husband married again soon afterwards and James never did return but eventually died in Ireland in 'penury and wretchedness'. As late as the mid-nineteenth century Marjorie's ghost, clad in a dress with green sleeves, was said to haunt the room where she had died.[8]

DISCOVERED LIVES

¹ Louisa G. Graeme, *Or and Sable: A Book of the Graemes and Grahams* (Edinburgh 1903), 49, 80, 91, 102 (an enthusiastic but not always accurate family history which wrongly refers to her as Marion.)
² *Handbook of British Chronology*, 196; Brunton, *Lords of Session*, 252-253; G. G. Smith, 'Oliphant, Sir William, Lord Newton', rev. John Finlay, *ODNB* (Oxford University Press 2004)
³ *Edinburgh Housemails Taxation Book, passim*
⁴ ECA, MS Dean of Guild Accounts 1626-1720, 1631-32, n/p
⁵ Graeme, op. cit., 101-103
⁶ John Riddell, *Inquiry into the Law and Practice in Scottish Peerages, Before and After the Union* (Edinburgh 1842), 227; *Scot of Scotstarvet*, 109; Brunton, *Lords of Session*, 282; Graeme, op. cit., 102
⁷ Brunton, *Lords of Session*, xviii, 282
⁸ Riddell, op. cit., 224-227; M.P. Brown, *Supplement to the Dictionary of the Decisions of the Court of Session*, i, (Edinburgh 1826), 30; Graeme, op. cit., 102-103; Scot of Scotstarvet, 109

# 38

## *Sophia Hume, Mrs Johnston*

Sophia Hume was the youngest daughter of the redoubtable Juliana Ker **(13)** and Sir Patrick Hume of Polwarth, the well-known Court poet.[1] She was born before 1609,[2] and we know that by 1631-32 she was the wife of Mr Joseph Johnston. In that year her seat in St Giles' was being faced with fashionable wainscot, presumably in order to improve its appearance.[3] Another member of the wealthy Johnston family of merchants, her husband was the son of that prominent holder of conventicles Rachel Arnot, the brother of Janet Johnston **(29)** and the uncle of the famous Archibald Johnston of Warriston.

Joseph was his parents' youngest son. He had still been a minor when his father made his Will in 1618, giving instructions that the boy was to be his executor once he came of age, remaining with his mother until then. He was to be suitably educated, and when he reached the age of twenty-one he was to inherit 5000 merks.[4] This choice of executor is interesting, for he had an elder brother, Samuel, who would have a flourishing career as an advocate and might have been a more obvious choice, but Samuel would inherit his father's properties, and their parents obviously wished to ensure that their younger son was provided for too.

Rachel evidently sent Joseph to university, his title of 'Master' indicating that he was a graduate, and he seems to have inherited a considerable amount of money and property from her when she died in 1626. The ready money lying in her house at the time of her death was the surprisingly large amount of £2912, and the total of her moveables came to £6322. The list of people owing her money at the time of her death included Sophia's mother Juliana Ker and step-father, who had jointly been renting from Rachel an expensive chamber in the centre of Edinburgh. They would not have lived there, for it consisted of only one room, but it was probably where they did the business of their various estates.[5] Joseph's brother Samuel duly inherited Sciennes from his father but Joseph received from his mother the estate of Hilton in Berwickshire, originally purchased by Rachel's father.[6] Rachel probably bequeathed to him some of her Edinburgh houses too, for that same year he was able to afford to lend 10,000 merks to Edinburgh Town Council, which was repaid to him the following year.[7]

By the mid-1630s Sophia and her husband were living in a substantial house which he owned near St Giles', on what would become the site of the Tron Kirk, and he rented out various other houses and shops in the area.[8] Sophia and he would also have spent time at Hilton, an area that she would have known well when she was growing up at her parents' country home, Redbraes Castle near Duns.[9] Her husband farmed the Mains of Hilton, or more likely employed a farm manager, growing wheat, oats and barley, raising sheep and keeping oxen for the ploughing.[10]

The exact number of Sophia's children is unknown, but she had a daughter called after herself and several sons, the eldest of whom, Archibald, was apparently born in 1628.[11] A younger baby arrived in October 1635, when her husband was away from home, and Juliana Ker instructed Sophia's brother George to tell Master Joseph to stay where he was for at least ten or twelve more days, as Sophia would not be kirked for another fortnight at the earliest.[12] The churching of women had been a feature of the Roman Catholic Church for centuries, its Jewish origins deriving from the belief that a woman had to be purified after childbirth, which was the result of sexual activity. She was therefore not allowed to resume normal life, including marital relations, or enter a church, until the kirking service with its blessing from the minister had taken place a month after she had given birth.

A number of Presbyterians in post-Reformation Scotland objected to the kirking service as being 'popish', and it is surprising to find someone who had married into the strictly Covenanting Johnston family participating in the rite. Nevertheless it continued for a long time after the Reformation in the Church of Scotland as a service of blessing and thanksgiving for the mother's survival of childbirth, not least because women themselves liked it.[13] As late as 1703 the staunchly Presbyterian Anne, 3rd Duchess of Hamilton was remarking that her daughter Susan had indicated that she would go to church the previous day though her month was not yet out, since she was eager to get to Edinburgh before parliament met.[14]

Eighteen months after the birth of Sophia's final recorded baby, she was widowed. Her husband died in Edinburgh on 18 May 1637 and his testament was given in by his brother Samuel, acting for one of Sophia's minor sons who was to be the executor. Apart from a grey horse worth £80 which would have been the dead man's means of transport, and another horse and mare, one of them probably used by Sophia, the list of debts owed by her husband included a half year's fee of £50 due to Mr James Naismith, who was employed as pedagogue to the couple's eldest son, and half a year's fee of £20 owed to Annabella,

Sophia's gentlewoman.[15] A gentlewoman was not a maidservant, but more of a companion and personal helper of an aristocratic lady. Sophia was still alive in October 1638, but her own date of death is not known.

---

[1] *Scots Peerage*, vi, 10-11

[2] NRS, Wills and Testaments, Edinburgh Commissary Court, CC8/8/46/688-693 (Patrick Hume)

[3] ECA, MS Dean of Guild Accounts 1626-1720, 1631-1632 n/p

[4] NRS, Wills and Testaments, Edinburgh Commissary Court, CC8/8/50/424-427 (Archibald Johnston, merchant); *The Diary of Sir Archibald Johnston of Wariston 1632-39* ed. G. M. Paull (Scottish History Society 1911), xi, 7

[5] NRS, Wills and Testaments, Edinburgh Commissary Court, CC8/8/53/680 (Rachel Arnot)

[6] *The Register of the Great Seal of Scotland AD 1609-1620* ed. John Maitland Thomson (Edinburgh 1892), no. 1014, p.369

[7] *Edinburgh Burgh Extracts 1626-1641*, 4

[8] *Edinburgh Housemails*, 148, 152, 153, 163, 165, 377, 410

[9] *The Register of the Great Seal of Scotland AD 1609-1620*, no. 1014, p.369; Michael R. G. Spiller, 'Hume, Sir Patrick, of Polwarth', *ODNB* (Oxford University Press, 2004)

[10] NRS, Wills and Testaments, Edinburgh Commissary Court, CC8/8/59/23 (Joseph Johnston), 23

[11] G.E. Cokayne et al., *The Complete Peerage of England, Scotland, Ireland, Great Britain and the United Kingdom* (Gloucester 2000 reprint), i, 166

[12] NRS, Papers of the family of Home of Polwarth, GD158/2697/13/20

[13] David Cressy, 'Purification, Thanksgiving and the Churching of Women in Post-Reformation England' in *Past and Present*, no. 141, November 1993 (Oxford University Press), 106-146; Natalie Knödel, 'The Churching of Women', (University of Durham 1995), http://users.ox.ac.uk/~mikef/church.html#top; Margaret Houlbrooke, *Rite out of Time: A Study of the Ancient Rite of Churching and its Survival in the Twentieth Century* (Donington 2011)

[14] The Duke of Atholl's Manuscripts, 45 III 47a, letter of Anne, 3rd Duchess of Hamilton to her daughter, Lady Susan Hamilton, Lady Yester

[15] NRS, Wills and Testaments, Edinburgh Commissary Court, CC8/8/59/23-24 (Joseph Johnston)

# 39

## Margaret Livingston, Countess of Wigtown

In 1625 Margaret Livingston, Countess of Wigtown sat for her portrait to Adam de Colone, a Flemish artist who had recently settled in Scotland. He had already made a reputation for painting members of the aristocracy, and his presence in Edinburgh was particularly useful for their wives. Although the husbands could patronise the leading portrait painters in London, where they spent much of the winter at Court after 1603, most of the women accompanied them infrequently. Very often pregnant, they were unable to face the fortnight's journey there, jolting along in a horse-drawn coach. Now, Margaret would only have had to go to Edinburgh, or the artist may have come to her house. Wearing a dark dress, the sleeves slashed with pink, diamonds and a feather in her hair, a fashionable long earring called an earstring in one ear and a delicate jewelled pendant round her neck, she holds a fan in one hand and a carnation, symbolising love and fidelity, in the other. Plump and brown-haired, she was twenty-nine years old at the time, as the contemporary inscription on the painting helpfully records.[1] (Plate 8)

The younger daughter of Alexander, 7th Lord Livingston, a faithful supporter of James VI and a member of the Scottish Privy Council, Margaret's earliest years had often been spent in the company of two royal princesses. In 1596, when she was still a baby, James VI entrusted her parents with the care of his own first daughter, Princess Elizabeth, who had been born a few months earlier. In adult life, this little girl was known as Elizabeth of Bohemia, The Winter

Queen. Two years after her arrival in the Livingston household she was joined by her sister, Princess Margaret, who would die at the age of two.

That whole arrangement was the subject of fierce criticism because Margaret Livingston's mother, Eleanor Hay, had originally been a Protestant but had early on become a devout Catholic convert like her brother, the 9th Earl of Errol. The Church of Scotland therefore took great exception to James VI's daughters being given into the care of Eleanor and her husband. The King brushed aside the continuing objections on the grounds that Livingston was a reliable Protestant and Princess Elizabeth remained in the Livingston household for the next seven years until she was taken south when James VI inherited the English throne in 1603.[2] Meanwhile, Margaret's mother was in constant trouble with the local presbytery, but she was protected by her husband, attended the local church with him from time to time in an attempt to silence the complaints and her children were apparently brought up as Protestants, further to disarm the critics.[3]

In 1609 Margaret was married to John Fleming, who was six years older than she was and heir to the 1st Earl of Wigtown. Her tocher was a handsome 28,000 merks. Five years after that, Wigtown granted the couple his lordship of Cumbernauld, and they presumably moved into his principal residence, its medieval tower house, with their growing family. On her father-in-law's death in 1619, Margaret became Countess of Wigtown. She and her husband would have eight children, three sons and five daughters. The eldest daughter was four years old by then. When she was born, Margaret's only sister Anna, Countess of Eglinton, had been unable to attend the baptism because she was expecting her own latest child within the following week or so, but she had urged her husband not to refuse to go, 'although I know the bairn's name will be Eleanor, after My Lady, my mother.' He evidently would have objected to this compliment to his Catholic mother-in-law.[4]

Margaret's own religious beliefs were very different, for there is evidence that she was strongly opposed to Charles I's ecclesiastical policies in Scotland. The minister at Lanark was William Livingston, her fairly distant cousin and, throughout his life, a zealous opponent of episcopacy and ceremonies in the Church of Scotland. Born in 1603 his son John shared his father's views 'from infancy' and recalled that during his own teenage years 'sundry gracious Christians' went to Communion at his father's house, the first names on his list being Robert Bruce, former minister of St Giles', and 'the rare Countess of Wigtown'.[5] They were not Livingston's parishioners, but had deliberately sought out a service of which they approved.

Margaret enjoyed a close relationship with her sister, Anna, and a few of their letters to each other survive. One or two of these discuss a minor problem with a servant, but a letter from Margaret dated 12 August 1627 is much more significant. She was looking forward to Anna's impending visit with her husband. It was as well that she was coming, for their mother was now living with Margaret and Eleanor's health was very poor. She was more and more short of breath every day. Moreover, Robert Bruce was currently a guest at Cumbernauld. Margaret intended to keep him there until Anna came, for 'He teaches to My Lady [Eleanor] this forenoon' and Ladies Boyd and Kilsyth would hear him too, along with Kilsyth himself.[6] Like Livingston, Bruce was a relative, for he was Margaret and Anna's cousin. He had long since been removed from his position at St Giles' because of his energetic criticisms of

James VI's ecclesiastical policies, and although now living in retirement on his estate, he remained strongly opposed to Charles I's determination to retain bishops and, for instance, insist that people knelt at Communion in the Church of Scotland.[7]

Perhaps he was not available when Margaret's mother lay dying soon afterwards. At any rate, Margaret sent for John Livingston, explaining to him that Eleanor had been 'all her days a Papist but some while before had quit it.' He was twenty-three now and had managed to obtain a position as assistant minister at Torphichen, just six miles away. When he received her message, his employment had just been terminated and he was about to go back to his father's house in Lanark. However, he set off for Cumbernauld instead. Margaret sympathised with his difficulties in finding work as a minister and suggested that he stay on with her and her husband, preaching to them, their family and nearby churchgoers in the great hall of their house until he found a position elsewhere. Their own parish church was half a dozen miles away and so the local people would be glad to attend somewhere nearer, she said.

This he did, rather reluctantly, for more than two and a half years. In 1629 an anonymous book was published, entitled *The Confession and Conversion of the Right Honourable, Most Illustrious and Elect Lady, My Lady C[ountess] of L[inlithgow]*. The text describes Eleanor's conversion to Protestantism 'in her old days', and there has been much argument in recent times about its exact status.[8] Was it really a deathbed confession, dictated by the dying woman or simply invented by the suspected author, Livingston himself, to further his own career? Given the fact that if he did indeed compose it, he put it together when he was still staying at Cumbernauld, Margaret must have approved it or even suggested it. After that, he left to take up his desired independent career in the ministry, and when he eventually wrote his memoirs he included Margaret and her sister in his list of people 'eminent for grace and gifts'.[9]

Not until 1634-35 was Margaret's seat put up in St Giles', perhaps because she lived mainly in the west.[10] Charles I had arranged for St Giles' to become a cathedral in 1633, but she would have found there many other men and women who shared her opposition to his ecclesiastical policies. Her husband, a devoted royalist and keen supporter of the King during the Civil War, died at their home in Cumbernauld in January 1650.[11] Margaret's date of death is unknown.

---

[1] The painting is in the collection of the Tate Gallery, London, T13340

[2] *Scots Peerage*, v, 443-446; Rosalind K. Marshall, *The Winter Queen: The Life of Elizabeth of Bohemia 1596-1662* (Edinburgh 1998), 16-21

[3] Kate Aughterson, 'Livingstone, Helen, countess of Linlithgow *ODNB* (Oxford University Press 2004)

[4] *Scots Peerage*, viii, 549-550; William Fraser, *Memorials of the Montgomeries, Earls of Eglinton*, i, (Edinburgh 1859), 199

[5] 'A Brief Historical Relation of the Life of Mr John Livingston written by himself' in *Select Biographies*, ed. W. K. Tweedie (Woodrow Society, Edinburgh, 1845), i, 130-131; Ginny Gardner, 'Livingstone, John', *ODNB* (Oxford University Press 2004)

[6] *Memorials of the Montgomeries*, i, 218

[7] James Kirk, 'Robert Bruce, Church of Scotland', *ODNB* (Oxford University Press 2004-16)

[8] E.g. Sarah M. Dunnigan, 'Spirituality' in *The Edinburgh Companion to Scottish Women's Writing* ed. Glenda Norquay (Edinburgh 2012), 20; Pamela Giles, 'Helen Hay (Eleanor, Helenor)' in *The Biographical Dictionary of Scottish Women* ed. Elizabeth Ewan, Sue Innes, Siân Reynolds (Edinburgh 2006), 163-4; Aughterson, op. cit.

[9] 'A Brief Historical Relation', i, 341

[10] ECA, MS Dean of Guild Accounts 1626-1720, n/p

[11] Lamont, *Diary*, 17

# 40

## *Helen Sinclair, Mrs Hay*

Helen Sinclair was the eldest of the four daughters of Sir John Sinclair of Stevenson and his wife Marion Maknath.[1] Sinclair was an extremely wealthy Edinburgh merchant who served as Dean of Guild for several years, succeeding the even wealthier William Dick in that position in 1636.[2] Apart from his own large house in Edinburgh, on the south side of the High Street behind where the Tron Kirk now stands,[3] Sinclair also owned several other properties in the town, which he rented out.[4] In addition, in 1624 he acquired the house and estate of Stevenston in East Lothian, a mile and a half from Haddington, adding the fertile farming lands of Pencaitland and Woodhall in the same neighbourhood.[5]

We do not know the date of Helen's birth, or that of her marriage, but she was probably born in about 1606 and by 1626 she was the wife of William Hay, son of the well-known royalist judge John Hay, later Lord Barro, who took his judicial title from his family estate in East Lothian.[6] Her husband enters the records that year because he and Helen were able to lend 20,000 merks to Edinburgh Town Council, on the same occasion that their neighbour Joseph Johnston, husband of Sophia Hume **(38)**, lent the Council half of that amount.[7] The fact that the loan came from 'Mr William Hay and his wife' is significant. Helen's husband is said to have been only twenty-two at that time,[8] and as a younger son, he did not stand to inherit his father's wealth. Wives were never usually mentioned in such transactions, so a considerable part of the 20,000 merks would probably have come from Helen herself, either directly or more likely from the tocher she had brought to her marriage.

In that same document her husband is described as 'commissary clerk of Edinburgh'. The Church courts in Scotland after the Reformation, known as the Commissary Courts, were staffed by qualified lawyers and dealt with matters such as divorce, legitimacy and the registration of Testaments, so a commissary clerk, particularly in Edinburgh, was a more important position than its title might suggest.[9] Hay would later become one of the Clerks of Session who organised the administration of the Court of Session.[10] By the mid-1630s Helen, her husband and children were living in a large house rented from her father close to his own home.[11] They had three sons, John, Henry and William, and two daughters, Janet and Helen. The family were parishioners of St Giles', and in 1634-35 the Dean of Guild accounts note that Helen's seat there was given a lock, at a cost of £1:4/-. This could have been a finishing touch to a new seat, or her seat might have been constructed earlier, but had been in danger of being occupied or damaged by some intruder.[12]

The Sinclair and the Hay families continued to remain close and there is no sign that an unfortunate rivalry in 1637 damaged the relationship. That year Helen's father stood as a candidate to be Lord Provost of Edinburgh but failed to be elected because her father-in-law, who had been recommended by Charles I, was successful instead.[13] At some point, Helen's husband acquired the lands of Aberlady in East Lothian, featuring in several of the later records as 'Mr William Hay of Aberlady', and their younger sons seem to have carried on the family's employment tradition, Henry becoming joint commissary clerk with his father and William achieving the position of Dean of Guild.[14]

Helen's father died in 1650, leaving not only his properties but the impressively large sum of £70,953, most of it in bonds, while his debts amounted to only £277, the fees owed to his eight male and five female servants for that year. He does not mention Helen in his Will, but her husband was one of his four sons-in-law who were to look after the interests of his young grandson, who was his heir.[15] Helen's father-in-law, Lord Barro, died four years later. He had joined the royalist side in the First Bishops' War and had later been captured fighting at the Battle of Philiphaugh in 1645. However, he was later released from prison and had been living in retirement in Duddingston.[16]

Helen's husband died in February 1656. A short omission from his principal testament was registered by his eldest son, Mr John Hay of Aberlady, nearly twenty years later, in 1674, but regrettably there seems to be no trace of the principal testament itself. However, the additional amount officially noted was not to be divided up in any way, which suggests that Helen herself had died by that time.[17]

---

[1] Richard Augustin Hay, *Genealogie of the Hayes of Tweeddale* ed. James Maidment (Edinburgh 1835), 42

[2] *Edinburgh Burgh Extracts 1626-41*, 182

[3] *Edinburgh Housemails Taxation Book*, 395

[4] Ibid., 392

[5] *Dictionary of the Decisions of the Court of Session*, Branch I of Appendix II ed. William Maxwell Morison (Edinburgh 1815), 397

[6] J.A. Hamilton rev. A.J. Mann, 'Hay, Sir John, Lord Barro (1578-1654)', *ODNB* (Oxford University Press 2004); Hay, *Genealogie*, 41

[7] *Edinburgh Burgh Extracts 1626-1641*, 4

[8] John Burke, *A Genealogical and Heraldic History of the Commoners of Great Britain and Ireland* (London 1837), 436

[9] Gordon Donaldson, *The Sources of Scottish History* (Edinburgh 1978), 28-29

[10] NRS, Wills and Testaments, Edinburgh Commissary Court, CC8/8/75/295-96 (William Hay of Aberlady)

[11] *Edinburgh Housemails Taxation Book*, 392

[12] ECA, Dean of Guild MS Accounts 1626-1720, 1634-35, n/p

[13] *Edinburgh Burgh Extracts 1626-1641*, 194

[14] NRS, Wills and Testaments, Edinburgh Commissary Court, CC8/8/75/295-296 (William Hay of Aberlady); Hay, *Genealogie*, 42-43; *The Records of the Parliaments of Scotland to 1707*, K.M. Brown et al eds (St Andrews, 2007-17), NAS, PA2/26, 101-12

[15] NRS, Wills and Testaments, Edinburgh Commissary Court, CC8/8/65/75-83 (Sir John Sinclair of Stevenston)

[16] Hamilton, 'Sir John Hay', *ODNB* (Oxford University Press 2004); *The Lord Provosts of Edinburgh*, 40

[17] NRS, Wills and Testaments, Edinburgh Commissary Court, CC8/8/75/295-296) (William Hay of Aberlady)

# 41

## *Margaret Hay, Lady Innerpeffer*

Margaret Hay was the younger daughter of Patrick Hay of Rattray and Margaret Boyd. Her father does not seem to have had a prominent public career, but he acquired various additional lands in Angus and Perthshire.[1] The dates of birth of his children have not been recorded, but judging by what we know of Margaret's future, she was possibly born in the 1590s and around 1610 married Sir Andrew Fletcher, son of a Dundee merchant burgess. He was a lawyer and, perhaps propelled forward by Margaret's prestigious uncle, George Hay, 1st Earl of Kinnoull, Lord Chancellor of Scotland, in 1623 he became a Court of Session judge with the title of Lord Innerpeffer.[2] Margaret and he had at least four children, Robert, Andrew, Jean and Beatrix. By 1634-36 he was renting a substantial house in the area behind what would become the site of the Tron Kirk and in 1634-35 Margaret had her seat in St Giles', its lock being added at a cost of 8 shillings.[3]

Details of her life are few and far between, but her husband was very wealthy and we know that she was fashionably dressed. The Scottish sumptuary laws stipulated what sort of clothes must be worn by the different sections of society, but certain favoured groups such as Edinburgh's Lord Provosts and the Lords of Session and their wives had the freedom to wear almost all fabrics, apart from cloth of gold or silver and similar lace.[4] Fortunately, several receipts for Margaret's purchases of materials and accessories have survived in the Fletcher family archives, giving us a glimpse of her appearance.[5] In June 1632, for instance, she was purchasing various items from William Caldwell, an Edinburgh merchant burgess. Along with quantities of fine linen, possibly for the undergarment known as a chemise, or for nightwear, she chose red ribbons, blue ribbons, silk lace and a pair of women's red stockings costing £2.

In winter, her rooms would have been chilly despite blazing fires in the hearths, and the black figured velvet she selected in December of that year would have been for a dress or an indoor gown, the garment worn over a dress and resembling a long coat. Cloaks were worn out of doors. Figured fabrics were reserved for those of the highest status. Besides the dress material, she purchased black buckram for lining, black ribbons and no fewer than 15 dozen little buttons, which formed decorative features of clothing at that time. These purchases might have been for a mourning garment, but black could still be a fashionable choice, as in the sixteenth century, although under the influence of Queen Henrietta Maria, paler shades were now becoming more popular. In summer, of course, lighter fabrics were appropriate and in July 1633 Margaret was buying 10 ells of flowered satin, at a cost of £80, along with £18 worth of silk lace to trim it. Again, flowered materials were forbidden to all but the most privileged groups.

A short bill in November 1633 from another merchant, Henry Inglis, was for a waistcoat (for a woman), buckram and braid, and it has a particularly interesting addition in the form of some Naples lace costing 45 shillings. Until then, Margaret was thought to have had only one daughter, Beatrix, but this bill plainly says that the lace is 'for your daughter Jean'. Another entry records the charges for silks for Margaret's gowns, with buckram to line her daughter's satin sleeves and for Jean's black gown. Finally, in April 1636, John Inglis was supplying items ordered by a letter from Margaret, who must have been out of town at the time. These consisted of six dozen silver plated buttons costing £4, a neck button with silver head and loop at 20 shillings and a silver belt at £4. There is no indication of which tailors made up her garments for her, but when she was at home, she obviously sat in St Giles' in expensive outfits befitting her husband's prominent position.

Meanwhile, his career was going from strength to strength. A committed supporter of Charles I, in January 1642 he was made Lord President of the Court of Session.[6] The following year, he purchased Saltoun Hall, at that time a tower house. Six miles south of Haddington, its spacious grounds had extensive views towards Soutra Hill.[7] His continuing support of the royalist cause, however, had a disastrous effect on his career. He subscribed £8500 towards the unsuccessful Engagement Campaign of 1648 which attempted to rescue Charles I from the Cromwellians, and as a result was dismissed from his position as a Lord of Session the following year.[8]

Reverting to his former title of Sir Andrew Fletcher, he made his Will at Saltoun on 21 March 1650.[9] He was, he said, weak and infirm in body but perfect and sound in mind and judgment. Knowing the certainty of his own mortality, he recommended his soul to his Creator, hoping for eternal salvation through the merits of Christ, and nominated his eldest son, Sir Robert Fletcher, as his only executor. He died an extremely wealthy man, leaving moveable goods and debts owing to him totalling £90,760, in addition, of course, to his various properties. All of this was to go to his eldest son, Sir Robert Fletcher, who was to pay to Andrew Fletcher, the second son and to Beatrix

Fletcher, 'his only daughter', the sums specified in the bonds of provision he had made for them. Jean must have died by then. He added that Andrew and Beatrix must accept the sums he had provided for them in full satisfaction of all they could claim by his decease, or by the decease of their late mother. Margaret's date of death is unknown, and she has been almost entirely forgotten, apart from a very occasional mention of her as the grandmother of Andrew Fletcher of Saltoun, the politician who would be a famous opponent of the 1707 Union of Scotland and England.

---

[1] *Scots Peerage*, v, 229-30; J.A. Hamilton, 'Fletcher, Sir Andrew of Innerpeffer, Lord Innerpeffer), rev. John R. Young, *ODNB* (Oxford University Press 2004)

[2] *Scots Peerage*, v, 220-223

[3] *Edinburgh Housemails Book*, 379; ECA, MS Dean of Guild Accounts 1626-1720, n/p 1634-35

[4] Frances J. Shaw, 'Sumptuary Legislation in Scotland' in *The Juridical Review: The Law Journal of Scottish Universities* (Edinburgh 1979), part 2, 84, 85, 87

[5] NLS, Fletcher of Saltoun Papers, MS 1706, 155, 158-9, 160-161, 165-166

[6] Hamilton, 'Fletcher, Sir Andrew, of Innerpeffer', *ODNB* (Oxford University Press 2004)

[7] Saltoun Hall, http://portal.historicenvironment.scot/designation/GDL00336

[8] Hamilton, 'Fletcher, Sir Andrew, of Innerpeffer', *ODNB* (Oxford University Press 2004)

[9] NRS, Wills and Testaments, Edinburgh Commissary Court, CC8/8/65/511-514 (Andrew Fletcher)

# 42

## *Mary Erskine, Countess Marischal*

Mary Erskine was the eldest daughter of John, 18th Earl of Mar who had been educated with James VI and remained his close friend, serving as Lord High Treasurer of Scotland from 1616 until 1630.[1] Her mother, Lady Marie Stewart, was the daughter of another of the King's most trusted subjects, his cousin the 1st Duke of Lennox.[2] Mary seems to have had a happy childhood with her older half-brother, seven brothers and four younger sisters. Their father was Keeper of the royal castle of Stirling, and he made his home there with his family. In his Will of 1634, he remarked rather touchingly that he and his dear wife regarded their loving children as their chief blessing in life, living together as they did in the peace of God. He went on to leave his soul to God and his heart to his gracious sovereign, King Charles I, whom he beseeched to be the protector of his wife and children, especially Willie, the youngest. His other sons and daughters were grown up by then. The Earl died at the end of that same year.[3]

In 1609, apparently when she was only twelve, the earliest legal age for a girl to marry, Mary had become the wife of William Keith, who was in his early twenties and would become 6th Earl Marischal in 1623, in succession to his father.[4] Marriages of that description were still taking place in order to further political alliances, but like other child brides, Mary would probably have remained with her own family until she was fifteen or sixteen and physically mature enough to have children. By her marriage contract, the lands of Fetteresso with its medieval tower house, just west of Stonehaven in Kincardineshire, were settled upon her, but once they were living together she and her husband occupied as their main residence the formidable, dramatically placed and lavishly furnished Dunottar Castle on its towering cliff high above the North Sea.[5] (Plate 10)

An inventory of the castle in 1612 notes that it contained no fewer than forty-one sets of tapestries, each set consisting of five or six panels. Of course that does not imply that there were forty-one principal rooms at Dunottar. Some of the tapestries would have been old and out of fashion and some would be brought out only for particular occasions, such as funerals. However, the collection was a splendid one, and included a magnificent gilt tapestry, a set depicting the story of Samson and another with white satin embroidery. The four-poster beds had curtains made of taffeta and damask. Green was a favourite colour and many of them were richly embroidered with silk. The collection of silver was equally impressive, with double overgilt basins, ewers, goblets, salts, spoons and plates.[6] Five years later, Mary and her husband had the honour of entertaining James VI and I there, during his return visit to Scotland.[7]

In 1626 Mary had her portrait painted, possibly by the Scottish artist George Jamesone. Looking at the viewer with a mild and pleasant expression, she wears a gold-embroidered black dress with an elaborate ruff, a jewelled band in her hair, a very large diamond locket at the centre of her bodice and an elegant earstring with a tiny crowned heart hanging from her right ear.[8] (Plate 9) At that point her children were still very young, some not yet born, but she soon had to give her attention to a public crisis. In January 1628 the *Santa Maria*, a German ship named after the

179

principal church in its home port of Lübeck, was carrying back from Spain a valuable cargo of Malaga wines, raisins, sugars, sweetmeats and aniseed, which was used both for cookery and medicinal purposes. It was intercepted by several Scottish merchant vessels in the belief or on the pretext that the cargo belonged to King's enemies. They intended taking it to Leith, where they could sell its valuable cargo, but 'a tempestuous storm' drove the *Santa Maria* north and the vessel was wrecked on the shore near Peterhead.

The captain and crew survived and were provided with food and clothing, but the local people swooped down and purloined a significant amount of the cargo. The Privy Council wanted to have the wreck and its contents brought to Leith, and as it was in the area owned by the Earl Marischal, who had a certain responsibility for Scottish and English shipping, they sent word that he must take charge of the arrangements. The Earl was away from home and could not be reached, so Mary rode the fifty miles from Dunottar to another of the family castles at Inverugie, which was close to the scene of the wreck. Intelligent and possessed of organisational skills, she took charge of the situation, and found 160 large barrels of wine, more than 60 casks of syrup and sugar, 60 barrels and 200 baskets of raisins and twenty pokes of aniseed.

She ordered all the wines to be tasted so as to separate from the rest those which had been spoiled with salt water. She then had 'a timber house' built to store the wine in, posting a guard around it so that no more could be stolen. Most of the raisins and aniseed were all wet too, so she had them moved to dry lofts to see if they could be saved. The sugar and syrup she put into safe keeping. She personally made an inventory of everything, and sent it to the Privy

Council, requesting that she be allowed to keep the goods where they were until such time as her husband could tell her what to do with them. He still seems to have been absent from home when a petition was sent to the Privy Council on behalf of Mary and himself, claiming that the wreck and its contents were his, because of its location on his shore.

Ignoring this, the Privy Council thanked Mary warmly for all her efforts and her great expense, but instructed her to hand everything over to William Dick and William Gray, the Edinburgh merchant burgesses whom they were sending north for the purpose of bringing the valuable cargo to Leith, where they expected it to fetch £24,000 Scots. They promised to reimburse Mary for her expenses but in March, after further arguments, Charles I himself gave orders that the wreck and its contents in fact belonged to the Lord High Admiral of Scotland, Alexander, 2nd Earl of Linlithgow, because he had the right to all foreign prizes, in other words, ships captured by the Scots.[9]

Back home again, Mary continued to add to her family. As far as we know, she had at least seven sons and three daughters. The names of the sons are not all recorded, but John was said to be the seventh and youngest of the boys. The unrecorded two probably died in childhood, and several of the others had mental health problems in adult life. Robert, born in the early 1620s, graduated from Aberdeen University and had a career in the French army, but in his thirties was officially found to be 'destitute of his natural wit, furious [meaning deranged] and a natural idiot'. His next brother Alexander was also described tersely as 'an idiot'.[10] Their eldest sister, Mary, was married in 1632 to John Graham, Lord Kilpont. After he was stabbed to death in 1644 by a drunken comrade in Montrose's army, his wife 'fell into a distracted state' and by 1652 her mother was noted as being the official guardian of Lady Kilpont's jointure lands.[11] Given that both Robert and Lady Kilpont had apparently led normal lives in their younger years, they may perhaps have suffered from what we would now term post-traumatic distress disorder.

Meanwhile, Mary's husband died in Dunottar Castle on 28 October 1635, aged about fifty.[12] Shortly afterwards, there is evidence of her support for the opponents of bishops within the Church of Scotland, despite her royalist background. Samuel Rutherford, the significant Covenanting minster of Anworth in Kirkcudbrightshire, was in 1636 deprived of his position because of his opposition to Charles I's ecclesiastical policies and exiled to Aberdeen.[13] While there, he noted in a letter to Lady Kenmure (43) that the Countess Marischal and her Covenanting son William, the 7th Earl, were very kind to him and in another letter mentioned that her daughter, Lady Jean, was the enthusiastic patron of the Covenanting minister of Pitsligo, Andrew Cant.[14] In 1636-37, there is a reference to Mary's desk in the Auld Kirk of St Giles'. How long her seat had been there is uncertain, but it must have been her habit to attend the St Giles' services when she was in Edinburgh.[15] She was still busy with the affairs of her jointure lands at that point, but she seems to have left them largely to her legal representatives when any problem arose.[16]

In 1638 she married for a second time. Patrick Maule, her new husband, was a widower twice over, in his early fifties. A devoted royalist, he opposed the Covenanters and in 1646 was created Earl of Panmure by Charles I. As Mary explained in the marriage contract, which she herself wrote out, their intention was 'without worldly ends, and merely from a religious affection', so that they could 'live together and enjoy the company and conversation of each other.' They both had children and grandchildren, and sufficient means of their own, so they would not be burdensome to each other and would each pay half of their household expenses.[17] The following year Mary received a royal warrant allowing her to retain the title and status of Countess Marischal.[18] Her husband attended Charles I during the King's captivity in Carisbrooke Castle until the English parliament forced him to leave and after the King's execution, Mary and he lived quietly at Bolshan Castle, near Brechin, at that time his principal residence.[19]

Mary herself was caught up in the dramatic events following the execution of the King. Her eldest son William was captured by the Cromwellian army and imprisoned in the Tower of London in August 1651. He was the official keeper of the Scottish crown jewels ('The Honours of Scotland') when these were not in Edinburgh during sessions of the Scottish Parliament and he kept them locked up in a secure room in Dunottar Castle. He managed to send a messenger to his mother with the key. She set off at once from Bolshan for Dunottar, reaching there just a couple of hours before Cromwell's army arrived to besiege the castle. Mary gave the key to George Ogilvie, who was guarding the castle for her son with forty soldiers.

Ogilvie's wife and Christian Fletcher, wife of James Grainger the local minister of nearby Kinneff, devised a plan, smuggled out the crown jewels, and the minister hid them beneath the floor of his church. Grainger reported all this to Mary in case he died before they were retrieved. The crown and sceptre were just below the front of the pulpit, and the sword of state was at the west end, beneath the floor where many of the seats were. Dunottar Castle fell to the Cromwellian army after a siege of eight months, but the Honours of Scotland were safe. In 1655 the exiled Charles II wrote Mary an enthusiastic letter of thanks for her part in their preservation. With the Restoration, the crown jewels were finally delivered to her son the Earl Marischal, after a series of quarrels between the Kinneff minister, whom Mary supported and Ogilvie, whom she criticised, over who should be rewarded for their safety.[20]

The Earl of Panmure died at Bolshan Castle on 22 December 1661 after a long illness and was buried without pomp or ceremony, as was his wish, in his nearby family vault at Panbride Church, near Carnoustie.[21] Mary survived him. It is sometimes said that she seems to have died five or six years later, but the fact that there was no mention of a division of his assets when his Testament was registered in 1664 may imply that she was already dead by then.[22]

---

[1] *Scots Peerage*, v, 621-622; *Handbook of British Chronology*, 182

[2] Marshall, Rosalind K., 'Stuart [Stewart], Esmé, 1st Duke of Lennox', *ODNB* (Oxford University Press, 2004)

[3] NRAS, Wills and Testaments, Stirling Commissary Court, CC21/5/4/420-435 (John Erskine)

[4] *Scots Peerage*, vi, 54-56

[5] *Register of the Great Seal of Scotland 1609-1620*, ed. John Maitland Thomson (Edinburgh 1892), 76, no. 204; J. Crabb Watt, 'Dunottar and its Barons' in *The Scottish Historical Review*, ii. no. 8 (July 1905), 389-405

[6] Crabb Watt, op. cit., 394-397

[7] Crabb Watt, op. cit., 391

[8] National Gallery of Scotland, *Lady Mary Erskine, Countess Marischal* by George Jamesone, NG 958, see Plate 9; Scottish National Portrait Gallery, *John Erskine, 2nd Earl of Mar* attributed to Adam de Colone, PG 2211

[9] *Scots Peerage*, vi, 55-56, 275-76; *The Register of the Privy Council of Scotland*, 2nd series, ii, (1627-1628), ed. P. Hume Brown (Edinburgh 1900), 55, 59, 189-192, 195, 198-200, 204, 219-220, 222, 232, 238-240, 274, 277, 298, 564-565

[10] *Scots Peerage*, vi, 56-57

[11] William Fraser, *Red Book of Menteith* (Edinburgh 1880), 508, 514, 574

[12] Ibid., vi, 56

[13] Coffey, John. 'Rutherford, Samuel', *ODNB* (Oxford University Press 2004)

[14] Vaughan T. Wells, 'The Origins of Covenanting Thought and Resistance *c.* 1580-1638' (University of Stirling Ph.D. thesis, September 1997), 126

[15] ECA, MS Dean of Guild Accounts 1626-1720; 1636-37, p.10

[16] *The Register of the Privy Council of Scotland*, 2nd series, vi (1635-1637), ed. P. Hume Brown (Edinburgh 1905), 344, 584, 631-633

[17] *Registrum de Panmure*, ed. J. Stuart, (Edinburgh 1874), vol. i, pp xlii-xliii; Andrew Jervise and James Gammach, *Memorials of Angus and Mearns* (Edinburgh 1885), 14-15

[18] Royal Warrant to Mary, Countess Marischal, 7 December 1647, http://manuscripts.nls.uk/repositories/2/archival_objects/6097)

[19] Douglas G. Barron, *In Defence of the Regalia 1651-2* (London 1910), 125; *Report on the Laing Manuscripts preserved in the University of Edinburgh*, (London 1914), i, 277-79, 282-83

[20] 'Papers relative to the preservation of the Honours of Scotland in Dunnottar Castle', 1651-2 in *The Diary of Sir Archibald Johnston, Lord Wariston. 1649, and other Papers* ed. C.R.A. Howden (Scottish History Society 1896); Barron, op. cit., *passim; Laing Manuscripts,* i, (London 1914), 277-113

[21] *Laing Manuscripts,* i, 282; *Scots Peerage*, vii, 94; Jervise and Gammach, op. cit., 14

[22] NRS, Wills and Testaments, Brechin Commissary Court, CC3/3/6/614 (Patrick Maule)

# 43

## *Jean Campbell, Viscountess Kenmure*

Lady Jean Campbell was the third daughter of Archibald, 7th Earl of Argyll and the cousin of Mary, Countess of Dunfermline **(45)**. Judging by the known age of some of her siblings, she was probably born about 1602, in the principal family residence of Inveraray Castle, Argyllshire. Her mother, Lady Agnes Douglas, was best known as the subject of 'Aurora', a romantic sonnet cycle dedicated to her by the poet Sir William Alexander, a family friend who had composed it in his youth before either of them had married. In addition to her two elder sisters, Jean had two younger sisters, but her mother died in 1607, not long after giving birth to Jean's only brother, Archibald, who would eventually become the 1st Marquis of Argyll.[1]

Whoever had the responsibility for bringing up Jean and her siblings after that is unknown, for her father was often absent and at one point was accused by the Scottish Privy Council of neglecting the affairs of his estates.[2] He had moved to London with King James VI in 1603 and after that was mainly at Court, apart from attending ruthlessly to his duties as Justice General in Scotland from time to time. His visits home decreased considerably after his second marriage in 1610 to Anne Cornwallis, a Roman Catholic English lady with whom he had eight more children. He was in Scotland in 1617 for a few months because of the King's visit, but after that he never returned. Having converted to Catholicism, he moved the following year to the Spanish Netherlands with his second family, entering the service of the Spanish King and finally retiring to London, where he died in 1638.[3]

Meanwhile, at some date between 1624 and 1626, Jean married Sir John Gordon of Lochinvar, who was about her own age.[4] This was a fairly late marriage for a woman in her social position, no doubt because of her father's neglect, and her bridegroom may even have been someone of her own choice. They settled down in his tower house at Rosco in the parish of Anworth, in the Stewartry of Kirkcudbright. He was a firm Presbyterian, opposed to the royal determination to anglicise the Church of Scotland's structure and services. As the patron of Anworth Parish Church, he was responsible for its rebuilding in 1626. Jean and he were regular attenders, and when the minister died the following year, her husband was instrumental in having Samuel Rutherford appointed to replace him.[5] Two years after that, Gordon was twice among a long list of men chosen to apprehend all Jesuits, priests and people who were found going on pilgrimages to chapels and wells in the area.[6]

By then, Jean had developed a deep and entirely spiritual relationship with Rutherford, who would become a leading opponent of Charles I's ecclesiastical policies, and when they were apart, they wrote to each other regularly.[7] None of Jean's letters to him exists, but forty-nine of his were carefully preserved by her, and form the largest number of his known surviving correspondence with any one individual.[8] From the advice that he offered her, many of her own preoccupations are made clear. Ever since childhood she had been troubled about her beliefs. Was she really one of the Elect, or was her unworthiness leading to her being rejected by God? This was a question which had perplexed many people in the aftermath of the

Reformation, and she often felt depressed, a situation which was poignantly intensified by her attempts to have children.[9]

From January 1629 until 1633 Jean had three little daughters who all died in infancy, and possibly a fourth baby too.[10] Each time Rutherford tried to console her, telling her on the first occasion that she must grieve without complaining, for her baby was not lost, but had gone on before, to be like a star, shining in another hemisphere.[11] On another occasion, he remarked that she must tell herself that it was better by far that her child was in God's keeping, rather than with her.[12] Despite his reassurances, Jean increasingly saw these deaths as additional proof that God was punishing her for her sins. Addressing her once as 'Noble and Elect Lady', Rutherford frequently urged her to concentrate on becoming the spotless and blameless Bride of Christ.[13] His consolatory letters may seem strangely worded to us now, but these were normal theological expressions in his day and it was not that he was unsympathetic. In the summer of 1630 he had lost his wife, who had died after a year's severely painful illness, by which time their two children were also dead, and he would later thank Jean for her kindness to him during these bereavements. In spite of her difficulties, she was not self-absorbed, and had a reputation for sympathetic involvement with her husband's tenants.[14]

In September of 1630, she and her husband moved to London for some months, so that he could pursue his ultimately unsuccessful claim to the earldom of Gowrie.[15] Dismayed at her departure, Rutherford warned her in advance that she was going to a country where the sun of righteousness did not shine so clearly as in Scotland, and on her return in 1631, he commented that now she had seen for herself how worldly glory was nothing but a vapour, a shadow, and foam on the water. Whether this was a reaction to what she herself had written about London or was simply his own view is not evident.[16] On their return, Jean and her husband lived in Kenmure Castle, his tower house twenty miles from Anworth, which he set about extending.[17] Rutherford was by then very taken up with the crisis in the Scottish Church, urging Jean to stir up her husband and her influential brother, the 8th Earl of Argyll, to support the Covenanters, and indeed he relied on her and her relatives to intervene on his behalf whenever he was in trouble with the Church authorities.[18]

Charles I visited Scotland in 1633 for his coronation at Holyrood, and so Jean and her husband travelled to Edinburgh, where the King created him Viscount Kenmure. He attended the meeting of the Coronation Parliament which followed. Charles was insisting that Scottish clergy should wear the same garments as those worn in the Church of England. Although deeply opposed to this policy, Kenmure nevertheless felt that he could not offend the King, who had so recently honoured him, by refusing to support him. Saying that his wife was ill, he withdrew and returned home.[19]

The following summer Kenmure was in Edinburgh again, but once more left early, this time because of his own illness. Suffering from a high fever, he managed to get home. Jean, heavily pregnant yet again, watched over him tenderly, summoned Rutherford to come and console him, and when it became obvious that he was not going to recover, she allowed numerous relatives, friends and all his servants into his bedchamber to say farewell to him. He died towards sunset on 12 September 1634 at the age of thirty-five, still regretting that he had failed to oppose

Charles I's ecclesiastical policies.[20] Writing to her two days later to offer further consolation, Rutherford told her that as she was now a widow she was free to make Christ her only husband.[21]

Shortly afterwards, Jean gave birth to a posthumous son, whom she named John. The baby was understandably a great source of anxiety to her, for like all her previous children he was delicate. She lost the personal company of Rutherford when the King exiled him to Aberdeen despite the attempts of her brother to intercede on his behalf. Her correspondence with Rutherford continued, however. He constantly enquired about her 'sweet child', but the little boy died in 1639, when he was four.[22] By then even Rutherford was finding it difficult to understand why Jean was being asked to endure so many cruel losses. It seems that she spent more time in Edinburgh after that, for in the year 1638-39 a door, a backboard of wainscot and a footboard were supplied for her seat in the Auld Kirk of St Giles'.[23]

The following year, Jean and Rutherford both married again. Now in St Andrews as Principal of New College, he and his new wife, Jean McMath, would have seven children.[24] Jean's second husband was Sir Harry Montgomerie. The twenty-six-year-old younger son of the 6th Earl of Eglinton, he was another supporter of the Covenanters and probably more than ten years younger than she was. After Glasgow University, he had completed his education in his late teens in 1632 by studying mathematics, fencing and dancing in France. Jean would have no more children, but he and she enjoyed a loving relationship which was all too brief, for he died on 3 May 1643.[25] He had made his Will the previous December, saying that she, 'my dear heart', was to be the only executrix of his goods. His friends must make sure that all the terms of his marriage contract were fulfilled, and he urged his father and all who loved him 'to be kind and loving to my dear heart'.[26] Her correspondence with Rutherford had continued intermittently, and he wrote from London to tell her how heartily sorry he was that she was deprived of such a husband and the Kirk of such an active and faithful friend.[27]

Two years later he dedicated to her his book entitled *The Trial and Triumph of Faith*. His own health was declining, his letters became few and far between as a result, and on 24 July 1660 he wrote his last letter to her, sympathising with her anxiety about the plight of her brother, now Marquis of Argyll, who had been imprisoned at the Restoration for his earlier opposition to Charles I. Rutherford died in St Andrews on 30 March 1661. The Marquis was executed just outside St Giles' on 27 May. Rutherford's widow spoke later of the kindness Jean had shown to her and her sole surviving daughter Agnes when her husband died.[28]

Jean seems to have spent her latter years in Edinburgh, supporting the Covenanting ministers, many of whom had lost their parishes as a result of their views.[29] One of them was Robert McWard, whom she had known ever since her days in Anworth. Banished to Holland, he was now the minister of the Scottish church in Rotterdam. She gave him financial assistance and when he told her that he was going to publish an edition of Rutherford's correspondence, she sent him the forty-nine treasured letters that she had received from Rutherford so that they could be included. The volume duly appeared in 1664.[30] That same year, John Fullerton of Carleton dedicated his book *The Turtle Dove* to her, a prose and verse meditation on grief.[31] Among her Covenanting friends was the minister John Livingston, another Rotterdam exile, who died in 1672.[32] Very frail by that time, Jean lived on until 1675, and was buried in Greyfriars Churchyard on 26 February.[33]

[1] *Scots Peerage*, i, 346-50

[2] Ibid., 348

[3] Ibid., 349

[4] Rosalind K. Marshall, 'Gordon [née Campbell], Jane [Jean], Viscountess Kenmure *ODNB* (Oxford University Press 2004)

[5] *Fasti Ecclesiae Scoticanae* ed. Hew Scott, ii (Edinburgh 1917), 385; James Anderson, *The Ladies of the Covenant* (Glasgow and Edinburgh 1862), 52

[6] *Register of the Privy Council of Scotland 1629-30*, 2nd series, iii, ed. P. Hume Brown, 239, 321

[7] John Coffey, 'Rutherford, Samuel', *ODNB* (Oxford University Press 2004)

[8] Anderson, *Ladies of the Covenant*, 67

[9] Andrew A. Bonar, *Letters of Samuel Rutherford* (Edinburgh 1904), *passim*

[10] Rutherford, *Letters*, 40-42, 46, 88, 97

[11] Ibid., 41

[12] Ibid., 88

[13] Ibid., 136

[14] Ibid., 4-5, 97

[15] Anderson, *Ladies of the Covenant*, 56

[16] Rutherford, *Letters*, 108

[17] Anderson, *Ladies of the Covenant*, 57

[18] Rutherford, *Letters*, 12, 88, 136

[19] Anderson, *Ladies of the Covenant*, 58; Gordon Donaldson, *Scottish Historical Documents* (Edinburgh 1970), 188-190

[20] Rutherford, *Letters*, 100-102, 609-610; Samuel Rutherford, *The Last and Heavenly Speeches and Glorious Departure of John, Viscount Kenmure* (1649)

[21] Rutherford, *Letters*, 100-101

[22] Ibid., 565-68

[23] ECA, MS Dean of Guild Accounts 1626-1720, 1638-39 p.14

[24] Rutherford, *Letters*, 16

[25] *The Register of Marriages for the Parish of Edinburgh 1595-1700*, ed. Henry Paton (Scottish Record Society 1905), 113, 486; William Fraser, *Memorials of the Montgomeries, Earls of Eglinton* (Edinburgh 1859), i, 76

[26] NRS, Wills and Testaments, Glasgow Commissary Court, CC9/7/29/232-234 (Henry Montgomery)

[27] Rutherford *Letters*, 609-610; Coffey, op. cit.

[28] Rutherford *Letters*, 698; Anderson, *Ladies of the Covenant*, 67

[29] Ibid., 76

[30] Ibid., 68-71

[31] John Fullerton, *The Turtle Dove* (London 1664), *passim*

[32] Anderson, *Ladies of the Covenant*, 80; Ginny Gardner, 'Livingstone, John', *ODNB* (Oxford University Press 2004)

[33] *Register of Interments in the Greyfriars Burying-Ground, Edinburgh 1658-1700*, ed. Henry Paton (SRS 1902), 355

# 44

## *Marion Brisbane, Mrs Colville*

Marion Brisbane's parentage is unknown, but she may have been a relative of the Brisbanes of Rosland in Lanarkshire, at least one of whom was an Edinburgh merchant.[1] She features in the records as the wife of William Colville (Colvin), a St Andrews University graduate who in 1635 had become minister of Cramond, at that time a separate village outside Edinburgh.[2] Since 1592, Edinburgh itself had been divided into four sections for ecclesiastical and administrative purposes and in 1639 the Tron Church was being built for the residents of the north-east quarter, which ran from opposite the east end of St Giles' down to the Netherbow. Colville was now appointed to be one of the two ministers of the Tron, but until it was ready, which did not happen until 1647, the congregation would occupy the Auld Kirk in St Giles'.[3]

It was in 1638-39 as Colville's wife that Marion was given her seat in St Giles'.[4] They seem to have been recently married, but in 1639 they suffered a prolonged separation, when her husband was sent by the Covenanters to seek the support of the French King, Louis XIV, in their struggle against Charles I's ecclesiastical policies. His journey was to take him south through England, but he only got as far as Newcastle, where he was stopped, his papers were seized and he was imprisoned. He was not released until August 1640, after the victory of the Scots at the Battle of Newburn.

He and Marion were reunited, and their eldest son John, who would become an advocate, was born the following year. Marion then had a second son, Alexander, baptised on 12 May 1643, to be followed by Janet in September 1646, Matthew in 1647 and Thomas, baptised on 27 May 1649.[5] Her husband's troubles were not over, however, for in July 1648 he was suspended by the General Assembly for having made plain his support of Charles I, and he was deposed on 26 July of the following year. He then went into exile in Utrecht, becoming minister of the English church there.

Marion had no more children after that. It seems likely that she would have gone with him to Utrecht, but no further mention of her has come to light, and it may be that she had died even in the short space of time between the birth of Thomas and her husband's departure, if not during their year in Utrecht. After that, Colville was allowed to return to Scotland, eventually becoming Principal of Edinburgh University and marrying his second wife, Marion Fyfe, in about 1654.[6]

---

[1] NRS, Wills and Testaments, Edinburgh Commissary Court, CC8/8/63/479-82 (George Brisbane)

[2] *Fasti Ecclesiae Scoticanae* i, 126, 134; A. S. Wayne Pearce, 'Colville, William', *ODNB* (Oxford University Press 2004); *Edinburgh Burgh Extracts 1626-1641*, viii, 162

[3] D. Butler, *The Tron Kirk of Edinburgh* (1906), 10, 188

[4] ECA, MS Dean of Guild Accounts 1626-1720, 1638-39, p.15

[5] *Fasti Ecclesiae Scoticanae* i, 134

[6] Ibid.

# 45

## *Mary Douglas, Countess of Dunfermline*

Mary Douglas was the third daughter of William, 6th Earl of Morton, Lord High Treasurer of Scotland, a close friend and supporter of Charles I. Her mother, Lady Ann Erskine, was a daughter of the 5th Earl Marischal.[1] Mary had five brothers and four sisters, and although her date of birth is not known, she was married in 1632 to Charles, 2nd Earl of Dunfermline. His mother, Margaret Hay, Countess of Dunfermline **(15)** was still alive, and Mary's marriage contract was careful to safeguard her mother-in-law's rights over certain aspects of the Earl's properties.[2] No doubt these clauses were inserted on the insistence of Margaret Hay herself. She and Charles had a difficult relationship. His very wealthy father had died when he was fourteen, leaving instructions that he should be brought up by his older cousin, George, 3rd Earl of Winton, who was to administer his vast finances. Winton did that meticulously and when Charles came of age, handed over the estates without any debts on them whatsoever.

In adult life, however, Charles was constantly being sued by his mother, who was intent on protecting her own liferent share of the Dunfermline properties.[3] Scot of Scotstarvet said that this was because of her son's financial problems, the result of his youthful gambling addiction as well as from other unspecified causes.[4] Seton family historians have severely criticised Margaret Hay for her attitude, but she may have had good reason to be wary. Her son would be severely in debt throughout his life, no doubt in part because of the political complications of the time, but despite generous gifts from the King. In 1650 he was owing no less than £77,000 Scots to John, 1ˢᵗ Earl of Tweeddale. By 1668, Tweeddale's successor had taken possession of Pinkie, Fyvie and Dunfermline as security for the debt, which would still be unpaid at the time of the Earl of Dunfermline's eventual death, when he left only £1648.[5]

Obviously these problems must have impacted on Mary's life. She had probably been very young when she married in 1632, and she and Dunfermline had three sons, Charles, born in 1640, followed by Alexander and James, and then a daughter, Henrietta in 1651. There were apparently other unrecorded daughters too, vaguely reported to have died young or unmarried.[6] Her husband also had an illegitimate son, Alexander. In a society where arranged marriages were the norm, it was accepted that husbands would have children from other relationships. These offspring were very often publicly recognised as theirs and well-educated. Such was the case with the illegitimate Alexander Seton or Ross (the latter presumably his mother's surname), who would graduate from university and become a leading Jesuit priest in Garioch.[7]

Unlike the royalist traditions of his own and Mary's families, Dunfermline signed the National Covenant in 1638, but during the Civil War he changed sides and after the execution of Charles I in 1649 he went into exile in Holland with Charles II, returning with him to Scotland the following year. Dunfermline was a great friend of the young King, and entertained him for eight or ten days.[8] Dunfermline Palace was actually the property of the monarch, and although Charles II had been born there, it had not been used as a royal residence after James VI and his family had moved to London. Whether the little Court was held there is not certain. They were possibly entertained instead at the Earl's nearby large house of Dalgety.

Anne Murray, a young Englishwoman of Scottish descent, had recently arrived in Scotland seeking respite from an unfortunate love affair, and had been accepted into Mary's household.[9] She has left a detailed account of her two years there, and so we know that during the King's stay at Dunfermline, Mary was one of those who had dinner or supper with him every day.[10] He left after almost a fortnight, but was back again shortly afterwards. However, when the Scottish army supporting Charles II was defeated overwhelmingly by Cromwell's forces at the Battle of Dunbar on 3 September 1650, Mary, like other members of the Court, sought safety further north, not expecting Cromwell's forces to follow.

With Anne Murray, Mary travelled to her husband's castle at Fyvie, about twenty-three miles north of Aberdeen. The roads in the north were probably not suitable for coaches, so they almost certainly rode on horseback and they took almost three weeks to get there. Setting off on 7 September, they went first to Kinross, and then to Perth, where the King now was, later stopping for several nights' rest at castles of Mary's friends and relatives, including Glamis and Dunottar. They finally arrived at Fyvie on the night of 27 September.[11] Its medieval castle had been very much extended and improved by Mary's father-in-law, but as she explained apologetically to Anne, it was in some disorder because it had not been occupied for some time.[12] Pinkie, close to Edinburgh, would presumably have been their usual residence. Even so, Anne later recalled that her own next two years at Fyvie were very happy. She was most concerned with her own situation, of course, but Mary features in her descriptions as someone kind, gentle and considerate.[13]

However, the danger had not passed, and when Charles II left for England, only to be defeated at the Battle of Worcester on 3 September 1651, Cromwell's forces marched north and reached Aberdeen.[14] The Earl of Dunfermline had not gone south with the King, but was at Fyvie. On hearing the news, he retreated into Moray. In his absence, the English army arrived and forced their way violently into Fyvie Castle, demanding supplies. Mary, who was heavily pregnant, was distraught, and with tears in her eyes, asked Anne if she would speak to the soldiers, since she, like them, was English. Anne bravely did so, demanding to know how they could think of threatening a heavily pregnant lady who had only women and children and just a few male servants with her. At this the soldiers said that they simply wanted food and drink and would not disturb the family.

Soon afterwards, three more regiments arrived. Mary invited Colonel Robert Lilburne and the two other Colonels to meet her in the castle dining room, promising that she would give them everything they needed if they would just issue her husband with a pass so that he could come back and be with her. Anne was present and had once been at a gathering which had included one of the Colonels, Thomas Fitch. Recognising her, and greatly surprised to find her there, he greeted her cordially, and promised to obtain the desired pass. As a result, Dunfermline arrived back in time for Mary to give birth to her sole surviving daughter, with the help of her midwife who had been summoned north from Dalkeith. Little Henrietta was named after Charles II's mother, Queen Henrietta Maria. Dunfermline left for Edinburgh to see to his business affairs as soon as Mary had recovered and the midwife rode south again, after being given about £120 Scots for her services and at the christening, which would have taken place shortly after the birth.[15]

This was not the end of Mary's difficulties. Colonel Lilburne became commander of the English army of occupation, and in June 1653 Mary was asking a family friend to speak to him about her situation. A captain and twenty-two English soldiers were now quartered at Fyvie, 'the most rude that ever I did see', she said. Their twenty-six or so horses were eating all her grass and to make matters worse the men were going into every room and taking away any of her belongings that they wanted to use. Her husband was in Orkney and she and her household felt like prisoners, for they could not go out or come back in without the soldiers' permission. She hoped that Lilburne could grant her an exemption from having his men quartered at the castle. Whether her plea was successful does not emerge from the correspondence.[16]

To what extent Mary was at Pinkie during these years is unknown, and the seat available for her in St Giles' seems to have varied. In 1618 her father-in-law, the 1st Earl of Dunfermline, had been granted a seat in the Auld Kirk for himself and his male heirs, with another built beside it for his wife and, in due course, for the wives of his son and their subsequent successors.[17] These two seats had been left to Mary's husband by his father, and that was where he and Mary would have sat when they attended St Giles' during the early years of their marriage. However, on 9 April 1644 the Earl decided that he wanted a seat in the East Kirk instead, and this was granted.[18] In 1658, he changed his mind and Edinburgh Town Council noted that he now wished to reclaim the Auld Kirk position which he had previously given up and so they appointed the Dean of Guild and two other colleagues to speak with him and find out exactly what he wanted.[19]

That was an unusual response, and there is no indication as to whether the request was granted. Leading members of the congregation sometimes had a seat in more than one of the St Giles' churches, but could these changes of mind on Dunfermline's part have been the result of his perennial disputes with his mother, Margaret Hay? Since she had officially retained her title and status as Countess of Dunfermline for life, she could have claimed that the seats she had occupied when her husband was alive were still rightly hers. Of course this is mere speculation and if there ever was a dispute of this nature, it ended in 1659. That year, Mary and her mother-in-law both died, Mary at Fyvie, Margaret Hay at some unrecorded location. They were buried in the family vault at Dalgety in Fife.[20]

---

[1] *Scots Peerage*, vi, 375-378

[2] *The Register of the Great Seal of Scotland AD 1620-1633*, ed. John Maitland Thomson (Edinburgh 1894), 709-710

[3] Bruce Gordon Seton, *The House of Seton, A Study of Lost Causes* (Edinburgh 1939), 307

[4] Scot of Scotstarvet, 47

[5] *The House of Seton*, 311

[6] *Scots Peerage*, iii, 16

[7] *The House of Seton*, 312

[8] *The Autobiography of Anne, Lady Halkett*, ed. John Gough Nichols (Camden Society 1875), 59

[9] David Stevenson, 'Halkett, Anne' in *ODNB*, (Oxford University Press 2008)

[10] *Autobiography of Anne, Lady Halkett*, 59-60

[11] Ibid., 62-64

[12] http://portal.historicenvironment.scot/designation/GDL00184; *Autobiography of Anne, Lady Halkett*, 62

[13] Ibid., 66

[14] Ibid., 66; John D. Grainger, *Cromwell Against the Scots* (East Linton 1997), 162-173

[15] *Autobiography of Anne, Lady Halkett*, 66-72

[16] NRS, Lothian Papers, GD40 Portfolio V, 60

[17] *Edinburgh Burgh Extracts 1606-1626*, 142

[18] *Edinburgh Burgh Extracts 1642-1655*, 49

[19] Ibid., 91

[20] *The House of Seton*, 312; Lamont, *Diary* (Maitland Club 1830), 119; Barry Coward, 'Lilburne, Robert' in *ODNB* (Oxford University Press 2004)

# 46

## *Marion McCulloch, Lady Stewart*

Marion McCulloch was the only child of David McCulloch and Margaret Elliott. He was a lawyer who owned the lands of Goodtries, just south of Edinburgh, now in that part of the city known as Moredun.[1] In the late 1630s Marion married John Elliot, a young advocate who may have been a relative of her mother and who rented from her father the lower part of McCulloch's house in the area between Greyfriars Church and the Grassmarket.[2] They had one daughter, Margaret, but Elliot fell ill in the summer of 1639, made his Will on 30 June and despite the drugs provided by Patrick Hepburn, apothecary, died in July.

He had probably been near the start of his career, but he left £1211:7/- worth of moveable goods, including his library valued at £40, and his clothing, household utensils and furnishings estimated at 200 merks. He and Marion had employed two servants, John Johnston and Agnes Howden. Marion was to register the list of his possessions, which she did six months later, but while he had spoken enthusiastically in his Will of his love for his brothers, she features only as 'his relict spouse', with no affectionate terminology. He made careful arrangements for their daughter, nominating Marion's father and probably his own father as her guardians during her minority, and Marion was to have the jointure (unspecified) which had been settled on her in their marriage contract. If their little daughter died, the money Elliot left was to be divided between his brothers and his wife.[3]

That did not happen, and Marion remained a widow for the next nine years until, late in 1648, she became the wife of Sir James Stewart, a wealthy forty-year-old merchant and moneylender who was a zealous Covenanter. Her tocher was the handsome sum of 10,000 merks and her new husband settled on her as her jointure £12,000 Scots, with the liferent of their house in Home's Close on the north side of Edinburgh High Street. He had previously been married to Anna Hope, a niece of the eminent lawyer Sir Thomas Hope, but for the past two years he had been a widower with seven children, the eldest now fifteen and the youngest about eight years old.

According to the nineteenth-century family historian, Stewart chose Marion because she was 'a grave matron, a widow of middle age, a woman of approved virtue and piety'. Despite allegedly being 'middle-aged', Marion then had four more daughters, Marion, Lilias, Catherine and Anna. The same family historian declared that the marriage was a happy one, thanks to Stewart's admirably urbane manner. He apparently knew exactly how to deal with his wife's outbursts, responding to her 'short sallies' by gently admonishing her and saying 'Insist, Marion', possibly when he was advising her on how to deal with her stepchildren. As a result, she would soon calm down and become 'all submission and acknowledgment'. Margaret Elliot, her daughter by her first marriage, eventually married Stewart's eldest son, Thomas.[4]

The year after her marriage to Stewart, he became Lord Provost of Edinburgh for the next two years and on 26 July 1650 he was granted for himself and his wife the seat in the East Kirk of St Giles', 'which they presently possess', under the King's Loft and close to the pulpit. The Town Council added cautiously that if the kirk were altered in future, they were to have whatever seat was in that position, and when one of them died, it should continue to be occupied by 'the longer liver of them.'[5] This uncertainty about the future arrangement of the seating was caused by the fact that the exiled King Charles II had arrived back in Scotland in the hope of reclaiming his throne. There were plans to move the Royal Seat in the Auld Kirk to the East Kirk, but no one knew what might happen next, and in fact Charles was defeated at the Battle of Worcester the following year. Scotland became an occupied country living under military rule, and Cromwell's second-in-command, Major General John Lambert, took over the East Kirk for his men, with English chaplains and ministers preaching there.[6]

In 1650 Stewart, the 1st Marquis of Argyll and the Earl of Eglinton had taken part in a conference with Oliver Cromwell at Bruntsfield Links, and Stewart continued to prosper, his Covenanting views making him acceptable to the new regime. He had purchased the lands of Kirkfield in Lanarkshire, now acquired the Coltness estate there,[7] and in 1659 he was elected to serve a second term of office as Lord Provost of Edinburgh.[8] With the Restoration, however, he was dismissed, and on 16 July 1660 he was imprisoned in Edinburgh Castle and then in Dundee, charged with not having kept proper accounts during the previous months of turmoil. A year later he was complaining to the Town Council that his seat in St Giles' had been given to Sir John Fletcher, the Lord Advocate.[9]

Despite producing careful accounts of all his financial transactions, he was accused of being responsible for the loss of £40,000 and permitting the execution of the Marquis of Montrose, which he had attended in his role as Lord Provost. Eventually, in 1669, he was told that he would be pardoned and freed if he paid a fine of £1000, but if he refused, he would be charged with treason. That would have brought with it the death penalty, and so he paid the £1000 and was released on 14 January 1670.[10] There is no record of Marion's life during those difficult years, apart from the fact that in 1662 and 1665, as her parents' only executrix, she registered the Testaments of her mother, who had died in 1660 and her father, who died in 1664.[11] When he was eventually freed, Stewart came back from Dundee and lived quietly in retirement. He died in his Edinburgh house on 31 March 1681 aged seventy-two and was buried beside his first wife in Greyfriars Churchyard. Marion lived until 1690, and was buried at Greyfriars on 2 July that year.[12]

---

[1] *Register of Interments in the Greyfriars Burying-Ground, Edinburgh 1658-1700*, ed. Henry Paton (Scottish Record Society 1902), 409; NRS, Wills and Testaments, Edinburgh Commissary Court CC8/8/72/31-32 (David McCulloch); ibid., CC8/8/70/676-677 (Margaret Elliot)

[2] *Edinburgh Housemails Taxation Book*, 558

[3] NRS, Wills and Testaments, Edinburgh Commissary Court CC8/8/59/342-345 (John Elliot)

[4] Archibald Stewart Denham, *The Coltness Collections* (Maitland Club, 1842), 27-28, 39, 342

[5] *Edinburgh Burgh Extracts 1642-1655*, 251-2

[6] *Coltness Collections*, 30-32; John D. Grainger, *Cromwell Against the Scots: The Last Anglo-Scottish War, 1650-1652* (East Linton 1997), 16-75; R. Scott Spurlock, *Cromwell and Scotland: Conquest and Religion, 1650-1660* (Edinburgh 2007), 7-38; Antonia Fraser, *Cromwell, Our Chief of Men* (London 1973), 258-60

[7] *Coltness Collections*, 341

[8] *Lord Provosts of Edinburgh*, 44-45

[9] *Edinburgh Burgh Extracts 1655-1665*, 247

[10] *Coltness Collections*, 38-39

[11] NRS, Testaments, CC8/8/70/676-677 (Margaret Elliot); CC8/8/72/31-32 (David McCulloch)

[12] *Coltness Collections*, 44; *Greyfriars Interments*, 410

# 47

## *Margaret Stewart, Lady Swinton*

Margaret Stewart was one of the eight children of William, 2nd Lord Blantyre and his wife Helen Scott. The family home was at Blantyre Craig, not far from Hamilton, in Lanarkshire. Margaret's father was a Justice of the Peace in Edinburgh in 1620, so he would probably have owned or rented a house there too. Otherwise his career seems to have been unexceptional.[1] He died in 1638 when Margaret would have been a young teenager and it was not until early in 1645 that she became the wife of John Swinton, who was a lawyer. Their marriage contract, in two parts, was signed on 28 December 1644 and 10 January 1645 and the next day, her bridegroom's father, Alexander, Lord Swinton, settled on her husband the lordship of Swinton, as part of the financial arrangements.

He mentioned in his grant that Margaret was marrying with the consent of 'certain of her friends', whom he did not specify, but said that they had been named in the marriage contract. In Scots the term 'friends' was often used to mean relatives and her brothers had probably been involved. That same day, in contemplation of the wedding, Lord Swinton granted Margaret the Mains of Cranshaws and some of its territories in Berwickshire, reserving to his own wife the jointure lands he had settled upon her when they had married.[2]

Margaret went on to have three sons, Alexander, John and Isaac, and a daughter named after herself. Their life was far from peaceful, however, for Swinton became very much involved in public affairs. He and his father were dedicated Covenanters, and both were on the committee of war for Berwickshire in 1646 and 1647. Her husband was bitterly opposed to the young Charles II, and after the Covenanters were defeated at the Battle of Dunbar in 1650, Swinton went to live in England. As a result, the Scottish parliament condemned him as a traitor, ordering his estates to be forfeited, and the Scottish Church excommunicated him.[3]

There is no evidence as to where Margaret and the children were living during his absence, but after the defeat of the royalist army at the Battle of Worcester in 1651 he returned to Scotland. The situation was abruptly changing with the invasion of Cromwell and the subsequent rule of the country by the English army. Swinton's opposition to Charles II was well known, as was his support of the National Covenant, and he had apparently made very important contacts with Puritan leaders when he was in London. Margaret now successfully petitioned Cromwell to have her husband's estates restored and he was appointed as one of the three commissioners for the administration of justice. Indeed, according to a leading contemporary, he was the man most trusted and employed by Cromwell.[4] In 1654 he once more became the M.P. for Berwickshire, and in that year we catch a glimpse of Margaret riding up the street in Edinburgh in 'great state' in a coach, as reported by Archibald Johnston of Warriston, who had been told about it by one of his friends. Johnston, although a leading Covenanter himself, was evidently one of the many Scots who loathed Swinton because of his previous defection to England and his subsequent closeness to Cromwell.

Eager to record the latest hostile gossip about Swinton, Johnston described the episode in his diary and, a month later, noted that Margaret was telling people that 'the Court' liked Patrick Gillespie the minister better than his fellow minister John Livingston. As with the report about her coach ride, this was taken to imply that she was inordinately proud of her new position and on this occasion was boasting to her friends about her knowledge of what was being said in privileged inner circles. This may or may not have been true. A couple of months later, Johnston's wife, Helen Hay **(48)** was telling her husband with some satisfaction that Lady Swinton had now been expressing much discontent and wished to be 'at their 3000 merks again,' meaning their former more modest lifestyle.[5]

Johnston also heard rumours that Swinton was failing to attend family services and playing cards instead. Margaret and he had probably both been members of the congregation of one of the St Giles' churches until his excommunication meant that he could no longer go to services. That was about to change, however. In December 1655 three members of Edinburgh Town Council were appointed to select a seat in the Tolbooth Church for Margaret's use. It was the church in the west part of St Giles' and it had recently been rearranged after being chosen as the one to be attended by the commissioners appointed by Cromwell to rule Scotland and the judges of the new Court of Exchequer.[6] The following March Swinton's sentence of excommunication was lifted.[7]

Everything seemed to be going well for him, but immediately after the Restoration of Charles II in 1660, he was arrested during a visit to London and charged with treason as a past opponent of Charles I. He was brought back to Scotland in company with the 1st Marquis of Argyll, who was similarly charged and then executed. Swinton, however, made such an impressive speech in his own defence that he escaped the expected death sentence and instead was imprisoned in Edinburgh Castle, forfeiting all his property and leaving him and his family destitute. Margaret was allowed to join him in the Castle, a not unusual occurrence when captives were well known people. She petitioned Charles II for assistance, explaining that she and her three sons were reduced to 'extreme poverty' and on 19 March 1662 the King granted them 40 shillings sterling a week from the Scottish Exchequer. Her presence in Swinton's company had fatal consequences, however, for she died in the Castle in December of that year, shortly after giving birth to their daughter Margaret.[8]

Swinton was eventually released in 1667 and in 1671 he married an Englishwoman named Frances Hancock. After his death early in 1679, she petitioned Charles II for assistance, having been left in 'a very poor and miserable condition.' In response, she was granted the pension which had never actually been paid to Margaret in 1662.[9]

---

[1] *Scots Peerage*, ii, 85-86

[2] *The Register of the Great Seal of Scotland AD 1634-1651*, ed. John Maitland Thomson (Edinburgh 1897), p.18 no. 2167; Archibald Campbell Swinton, *The Swintons of that Ilk* (Edinburgh 1883), clxxxviii-cxcii

[3] John Coffey, 'Swinton, John (c. 1620-1679)' in *ODNB*, (Oxford University Press, 2004)

[4] *The Swintons of that Ilk*, 66

[5] *The Diary of Sir Archibald Johnston of Warriston 1650-1654*, ed. David Hay Fleming (Scottish History Society), 269, 273, 315

[6] *Edinburgh Burgh Extracts 1655-1665*, 2-3

[7] Coffey, op. cit.

[8] Lamont, *Diary*, 158

[9] Coffey, op. cit. gives her surname as White, but the grant to her is printed in *The Swintons of that Ilk*, ccii-ciii, where she features as Frances Hancock

# 48

## *Helen Hay, Lady Warriston*

Helen Hay was the daughter of the judge, Alexander Hay, Lord Fostergate and his wife, Catherine Skene.[1] In 1634 Helen became the second wife of Archibald Johnston of Warriston, who would become a leading Covenanter. Five months after the death of his first wife in 1633, he had qualified as an advocate and decided that he must marry again.[2] Energetic, egotistical and painfully obsessed with his religious beliefs, he was terrified of choosing someone of whom God would disapprove. As he had done before his first marriage, he consulted all manner of friends and relatives, with the result that three possibilities emerged. The first lady instantly rejected his proposal, after which he struggled to choose between Catherine Morrison, the second daughter of Lady Prestongrange **(30)**, and Helen Hay. He rather inclined towards Helen, but changed his mind and listened to those who urged him to select Catherine. One of his brothers-in-law then declared that her family were proud and greedy, and he would not have a chance there, so he reverted to Helen.[3]

His courtship of her was prolonged and tormented. He still suffered all the doubts he had experienced before his first marriage, intensified by his grief at the recent loss of his wife. However, he finally proposed to Helen, pointing out to her all his faults. She seems to have fallen in love with him, for she accepted and then endured months of his further agonising, during which time he had long religious sessions with her almost every day, loudly weeping and wailing as he prayed. On his insistence, they studied the Psalms together, read the writings of Martin Luther, and attended services, he at least often hearing two sermons a day, in two different churches.

Helen went along with all that he advised, but even then he continued to suffer dreadful doubts, fearing that he had made the wrong choice and thinking that he must cancel his previous vows to her. He even complained to her that his 'inordinate affection' for her was disturbing his religious devotions and had further long consultations with his relatives, particularly his aunt Lady Curriehill **(29)**, who urged him not to change his mind. In addition to these anxieties, he was not well off financially and so there were lengthy problems in settling the marriage contract, but Helen and he were finally married in Currie Church on 4 September 1634.[4]

Their first child, Elizabeth, was born before August 1636, followed by a son, James, in 1637, who died in infancy, and then by Archibald, Rachel, Helen, Margaret, John, Alexander, Catherine, Anna and Janet, their final child, born in 1652, when Helen nearly died giving birth.[5] Meanwhile, Johnston became increasingly involved with public affairs, collaborating with Alexander Henderson, one of the ministers of St Giles', on the composition of the National Covenant and becoming deeply involved with the subsequent struggles against Charles I's desired changes to Scottish Church services. When the King came to Scotland in 1641 to try to conciliate the Covenanters, he knighted Johnston, and made him a Lord of Session. Later, he was given the position of Lord Clerk Register. Taking part in negotiations in England and spending lengthy periods in London as one of the commissioners to the Westminster Assembly, Johnston was frequently away from home. He lost all his public offices when the English occupied Scotland in 1651, but he soon found favour with Cromwell and regained his position as Lord Clerk Register once more.[6]

Intelligent and capable, Helen meanwhile brought up their children, reminded him to take his medicine and kept him in touch with all the latest news. When she heard that he was being criticised for some remark he made to Cromwell during what was described as one of his rambling discourses, she wrote to tell him that he must make sure that his sayings were to the Lord's honour and not to his own hurt. Her daily life became more and more demanding as he was so involved with his Covenanting campaign that he gave up his legal practice, which provided much of his income, and he was careless with their financial affairs. Desperately worried about their lack of money, Helen was often ill, her husband admitting on one occasion that her sickness was thought to be caused by anxiety, while she declared that the life of a common domestic drudge would be preferable to what she had to endure.[7] He was also quick to rebuke her sharply when, attending a wedding with 'her' daughter for a little light relief in 1654, the two had engaged in what he termed 'promiscuous dancing' instead of preparing for the following day's Communion service.[8]

Two years later, Helen had evidently written to Archibald, 1st Marquis of Argyll pleading for financial help for her husband. He was a family friend and their son Archibald was called after him, not after Johnston himself. Argyll replied to her, offering to arrange for Johnston to have a salary if he took the important early registers of the General Assembly of the Church of Scotland into his safe keeping. His previous discovery of them, with their Acts condemning bishops, had been instrumental in encouraging the opposition to Charles I's ecclesiastical policies. When Helen received his letter, she showed it eagerly to Johnston, but instead of gladly accepting the offer, he drafted a reply refusing it and insisted that she copy out his answer. This she did, weeping, and when he checked her letter to see that it was exactly as he had composed, he found her tear stained and sobbing bitterly, saying that she had wanted to describe their true condition and how they and their young family could not survive without help, but he remained adamant.[9] In the end, when Cromwell restored him to his position as Lord Clerk Register, he also granted him a pension, and Johnston then attended parliament in London. He continued to do so when Cromwell died and his son Richard succeeded him in 1659. Johnston now became Lord Warriston, President of the new Council of State.[10]

It was at that point, on 23 November 1659, that Edinburgh Town Council decided that the seat in the Tolbooth Church formerly possessed by the recent Lord Provost, Sir Andrew Ramsay, should now be assigned to Lord Warriston, his lady and his family.[11] Johnston had originally occupied a seat in the Auld Kirk of St Giles' in the late 1630s, but of course his children had very much increased in number since then. However, this improvement in the family situation did not last long. When he returned to Edinburgh in 1660 he found himself widely hated for his alignment with the English, and to add to Helen's troubles, their son Archibald was suffering from a severe mental illness, centring on his religious beliefs. Smearing his Bible with his own blood was one of his less extreme symptoms.

With the Restoration of 1660, an attempt was made to arrest Johnston for his opposition to Charles II, and he fled to the continent, disguised as a merchant.[12] During the next two years, much of the time spent in Hamburg, often in poor health, he received letters in cipher sent by Helen. These were intercepted and read by English spies. She also visited him on several occasions, both in Germany and when he subsequently moved to Rouen.[13] This had even more unfortunate consequences, for she had been recognised, followed and her husband was arrested. The French King, Louis XIV, was a friend of Charles II, and so Johnston, Helen and their daughter Margaret were sent to England where he and Margaret were imprisoned in the Tower of London.[14] When it was announced that he was to be sent by sea to Scotland for trial, in the spring of 1673, Helen petitioned the King for permission for herself and Margaret, 'now a prisoner with her father' to accompany him, since he was so ill with palsy [paralysis] and dropsy.[15]

Weak and mentally confused, he arrived at Leith in June and was forced to walk the long way uphill to his next prison, Edinburgh Tolbooth. He was sentenced to death, and on 9 June, Helen and the children petitioned the Scottish Privy Council, pleading 'with tears' for his execution to be delayed until he was stronger and had recovered his memory.[16] Their request was not granted, and on 22 July he was taken out to a high scaffold just outside St Giles', a few yards from the family home. His memory was suddenly clear and he made a calm, cheerful and lengthy speech, during which he commended his wife and children to his hearers, pleading for them not be ruined for his sake but instead 'favoured, assured, supplied and comforted'. Helen and the children would have been in the large crowd watching and listening. One of their sons, weeping, was on the scaffold with him when he was hanged like a common criminal, after which an executioner came forward to remove his head for display on top of the Netherbow Port. A short time afterwards, it was taken down, thanks to the intervention of an influential friend, and placed with his body, which had been buried in Greyfriars Churchyard.[17]

Helen lived on for another seven years. She had carefully kept her husband's diaries and other papers, and in the summer of 1670 she wrote a note transferring them to her 'dear good' son-in-law, Robert Baillie of Jerviswood, who was her nephew and had married her daughter Rachel.[18] She was obviously seriously ill by then, for her writing is very wavering. She survived for only a few weeks more, and the register of interments at Greyfriars on 7 September 1670 notes the burial there of 'Dame Helen Hay, widow of Sir Archibald Johnston'.[19]

---

[1] Brunton, *Lords of Session*, 244; *Memorials of the family of Skene of Skene*, ed. W F. Skene (New Spalding Club 1887), 112; *Scot of Scotstarvet*, 121-22

[2] *Diary of Sir Archibald Johnston of Warriston 1632-1639*, ed. George Morison Paul (Scottish History Society 1911), 10, 12-13

[3] Ibid., xx-xxi

[4] Ibid., xx-xxii, 187-246

[5] *Diary of Sir Archibald Johnston 1650-1654*, ed. David Hay Fleming (Scottish History Society 1919), 151-53

[6] John Coffey, 'Johnston, Sir Archibald, Lord Warriston', *ODNB* (Oxford University Press 2004)

[7] *Diary of Sir Archibald Johnston 1632-1639*, xxii-xxiii

[8] *Diary of Sir Archibald Johnston 1650-1654*, 297

[9] *Diary of Sir Archibald Johnston 1655-60*, ed. James D. Ogilvie (Scottish History Society 1940), 32-37

[10] Coffey, op. cit.

[11] *Edinburgh Burgh Extracts 1655-1665*, 175; *Lord Provosts of Edinburgh*, 45; J. Cameron Lees, *St Giles', Edinburgh* (Edinburgh 1889), 296

[12] Robert Wodrow, *The History of the Sufferings of the Church of Scotland* (Edinburgh 1828), 355

[13] Melinda Zook, *Protestantism, Politics and Women in Britain* (Hampshire 2013), 31

[14] Wodrow, op. cit., 355-356

[15] *Calendar of State Papers Domestic, Charles II,* (London 1862) lxxiii, 141

[16] *Register of the Privy Council of Scotland*, series 3, 1661-1664, ed. P. Hume Brown (Edinburgh 1908), 669-70

[17] Anonymous, *The Last Discourse of the Right Honourable The Lord Waristoune* (Edinburgh 1664), 7-11

[18] Facsimile printed in *Diary of Sir Archibald Johnston 1632-1639*, xi

[19] *Register of Interments in the Greyfriars Burying-Ground Edinburgh 1658-1700* ed. Henry Paton (Scottish Record Society 1902), 298

# 49

## *Marion Ellis, Mrs Hamilton*

By the 1670s, it had long been accepted that there would no longer be any segregation of the men and women of the congregations in St Giles', and instead families would expect to sit together, except in the few cases where a very prominent male member occupied a special loft with his colleagues. That, together with the strenuous but less than successful attempts of the Kirk Session to insist on the payment of seat rents, meant that the Town Council no longer received requests that some prominent women should be granted their own seats. The final application noted in such records came from a considerate husband concerned for his wife's future.

The parentage of Marion Ellis is not known, but various Edinburgh records list people of that surname.[1] Most of them were merchants, but there were a couple of advocates and one or two other lawyers. At some point, possibly around the 1640s, Marion married Mr Alexander Hamilton of Hill, Writer to the Signet. The eldest son of James Hamilton of Hill in the Lanarkshire parish of Bothwell, he had made his legal career in Edinburgh.[2] In 1632 he had been apprenticed for four years to James Kirkwood, W.S. When he completed his training he soon established himself and he then had an obviously successful career, for in 1654 and 1655 the commissioners for the administration of justice would appoint him, along with several others, as commissioners for the Writers to the Signet, with the condition that they must be resident in Edinburgh. On several occasions in 1655 he was one of those examining other Writers to the Signet who applied to become commissioners.[3]

Marion and he had at least four children. Their son Gavin was named after her husband's brother, who was killed in battle in 1645, and there were three daughters. Bethia would marry Thomas Moncrieff of that Ilk and her sister, whose name has not been recorded, became the wife of James Hunter, an advocate. Another daughter, Isabella, died in July 1660.[4] Marion's husband was still actively employed in 1671, when he had an apprentice and servant named Mr Thomas Gordon, but he died in March the following year.[5] He had prudently made his Will on 4 February 1670, and Marion registered it on 19 July 1675. By that time he had inherited the lands of Hill from his father, which of course were not included in his Testament, but his furnishings and his clothing were estimated to be worth £100 and no debts were owing to him. He himself owed £16 to each of their two servants for the year in which he died. John Foulis, apothecary, had sent in his bill for £20, the cost of the drugs and medicaments furnished to him during his final illness, and he owed £20 to 'the good town of Edinburgh' for the rent of his seat in St Giles'.

Recommending his soul to God Almighty, his creator, he asked to be buried with the faithful and appointed as his sole executrix 'my loving and dutiful spouse, Marion Ellis', leaving her his entire goods and gear, not merely the third part to which she was legally entitled.[6] He was buried in Greyfriars Churchyard on 2 April 1672, and on 6 December that year, Edinburgh Town Council noted that he had left 500 merks to the poor of the town, and had also desired that Marion might remain in possession of his seat in the East Church during her residence in the North East Parish, 'without payment of seat rent.' Perhaps in view of his charitable donation, his request was granted.[7]

Marion lived for almost thirteen years after his death, and was buried at Greyfriars on 13 March 1685.[8]

---

[1] e.g. *Register of Apprentices of the City of Edinburgh 1583-1666*, ed. Francis J. Grant (Scottish Record Society 1906); *Register of Marriages for the Parish of Edinburgh 1595-1700*, ed. Henry Paton (Scottish Record Society 1905); *Register of Interments in the Greyfriars Burying Ground, Edinburgh 1656-1700*, ed. Henry Paton (Scottish Record Society 1902)

[2] NRS, Wills and Testaments, Glasgow Commissary Court, CC9/7/25/359-361 (James Hamilton of Hill); John Anderson, *Memoirs of the House of Hamilton with Genealogical Memoirs of the Several Branches of the Family* (Edinburgh 1825), 303

[3] *A History of the Society of Writers to Her Majesty's Signet* (Edinburgh 1890), 265, 269, 274, 275

[4] *Memoirs of the House of Hamilton*, 303; *Interments in the Greyfriars Burying Ground*, 281

[5] *History of the Society of Writers*, 314

[6] NRS, Wills and Testaments, Edinburgh Commissary Court, CC8/8/75/327-329 (Alexander Hamilton)

[7] *Edinburgh Burgh Extracts 1665-1680*, 136; *Interments in the Greyfriars Burying Ground*, 281

[8] *Interments in the Greyfriars Burying Ground*, 206

# Index